TEN STEPS TO
PSYCHIC DEVELOPMENT

written by
Jacqueline Watson

TEN STEPS TO PSYCHIC DEVELOPMENT

ISBN 978-1-7330940-0-9

While the author has made every effort to provide accurate information at the time of publication, neither the publisher nor the author assumes any responsibility for errors.

Tranquil Spirits

Thank you
for choosing this book,
to guide you
on your spiritual journey.

Follow that dream.

INTRODUCTION

I taught psychic development for many years, and to hundreds of people before, my life changed and I started on my travels. Holding groups was no longer an option for me, and so I asked spirit what I should do next.

Their reply was, "Write a book."
"A book about what?" I asked.
"A book about psychic development," came their simple reply.
"But I don't know how to do that or even where to start," I answered feeling very bewildered. "All my teachings are in my head. I never wrote anything down."
"Well now is the time to write them down," they said, not taking any excuse for an answer. "Get your teachings out of your head and onto paper, exactly as you delivered each lesson. It is time to spread your word. It is time to share your gift with as many people as possible across the world."
"Ok, but you will have to help me," I reluctantly agreed.
"We will be right beside you with every word you write," came the very warm and welcome reply.

And so that is how I came to write this book - with spirit beside me all the way.

How do I know they were there?

Well, every lesson came easily from my head to the paper. If at anytime I felt I was struggling then I knew I was not connected to spirit but to my ego. When I let go of that, the words flowed and amazed me as I watched my fingers type.

I trusted and believed that with the help of spirit this book would be written to help and guide YOU to build your belief in spirit and yourself.

To assist you with your growth, there are exercises at the end of each lesson to help move you towards your goals faster. Practice, practice and more practice is essential here. I have also added some pages in each lesson, after each set of exercises, for you to write notes and keep track of your development.

As you begin, or continue, your spiritual journey know that you are on a great path with this book and your guides by your side.

Enjoy.
Hugs and smiles,
Jacqueline

You can contact me through my website
www.tranquil-spirits.com

CONTENTS

Chapter One
MY JOURNEY WITH SPIRIT

I believe events in everyone's life happen for a reason, and when the time is right for each of us.

When I started on my journey with spirit, it was most definitely the right time in my life and the reason became abundantly clear as time went by.

Although I maybe didn't realise it at first, spirit had always been around me and showed me some of the ways they worked, through members of my family. My nan, my mum's mum, used to read the tea leaves. When I was younger, now and then, she would do this for me, although not as often as I would have liked. She would always make tea using loose leaf tea from a special dispenser she had on her kitchen wall. She held the teapot underneath the dispenser and then pushed a button which released the tea into the teapot. She would push the button for the number of people who were having tea and then one for the pot! My nan always served the tea in china cups with saucers, and it was perfect every time. Although she used a tea strainer to catch the tea leaves, on the odd occasion a tea leaf would get into someone's cup and, without thinking, she would say something. For example, if there happened to be a tea leaf on the edge of the cup that would mean a letter arriving for that person or a floating tea leaf would mean a visitor. She especially loved to see lots of bubbles on the tea and would happily say that money was coming to that person

My nan only read the tea leaves occasionally and, as I grew older, I became more intrigued by them. If I managed to have my way, my nan would not use a tea strainer so that there would be tea leaves at the bottom of my cup for her to read. Of course I wanted her to do this all the time but she said she didn't like to read for family. This was a very normal response from people of her generation, as having any psychic skills was frowned upon. But on the few occasions I could talk her round, it made me even more curious to learn about them and today I really enjoy tea leaf reading or Tasseography, to give it the correct title.

My uncle Billy, my mum's brother, was a spiritualist healer and also channeled spirit. We didn't get to see him very often but when we did, I was fascinated with the way spirit would work with him. He would ask his wife for pen and paper at some random point during family activities and proceed to start writing, whilst staring straight ahead and using the opposite hand to what he normally wrote with. He wrote and published many of these writings, which were channeled through him from a Chinese man, and he also gave several talks on the radio. Eventually, as people near and far were learning of their skills, my aunt and uncle had a sanctuary built behind their house where people could go for healing.

As well as these two big influences in my childhood, my mum bought me my first pack of tarot cards when I was thirteen years old. Tarot cards have always fascinated me and I felt very honoured to actually own my own deck. Although I didn't really understand them at the time, I felt very drawn and connected to them, and experienced a sense of comfort when I was using them.

And so life went on for me. I married and had two children and experienced the ups and downs on my journey through life with spirit guiding me, although I was not necessarily aware of this connection. My tarot cards came with me wherever I went but I did not read them regularly, I just got on with my busy life.

It was in the year 2000 when I found spirit again, or I should say spirit gained my attention. I had been at a very low point in my life for a number of years and I eventually decided I needed to do something about it. So I turned my life upside down and started searching for happiness, a belief in myself and something new to focus on which could help to create this. A friend told me about a *Mind, Body & Spirit* event that was being held the following Saturday at a spiritualist centre not far from where I lived. I didn't really know what this was about but I felt curious and also something was telling me to go and take a look. So, with my daughter beside me, I decided to go along and investigate.

As I entered the large meeting room, along with other members of the public, I could see it was filled with different people demonstrating their work with spirit. There were card readers, healers, chakra balancers and many more. I must have looked slightly lost as I wandered around with my daughter, because eventually a lady came up to me and asked if I would like some healing. I responded by saying no thank you, as I wasn't poorly. I was very naive to spirit back then but luckily for me the lady said I didn't have to be sick to receive healing and continued to talk to me as she demonstrated a crystal healing on me. I am so pleased she did this as that started my true journey with spirit and I am happy to say I am now a spiritual healer, a Reiki master and a crystal therapist amongst other things.

My desire to learn the teachings of spirit started that day.

A lady called Lynn told me she was looking for new students to sit in a beginners group for spiritual development and, without hesitating, I added my name to her list.

The following week I started my first proper interaction with spirit and really haven't looked back. I sat in Lynn's group for a couple of years, learning different ways to contact spirit and how to give messages, plus I also took my spiritual healing course with her.

One day a friend asked me if I could teach her how to contact spirit. I told her I didn't teach and gave her Lynn's phone number. This continued over a few months with different people asking me to teach them. Eventually a lady asked me if I would teach her all I knew. She wouldn't take no for an answer and insisted she wanted me to teach her. I said I would think about it and get back to her. That night I asked spirit to guide me. If they wanted me to teach people, they had to send the students to me, as I did not have time to find them.

And so that's how it all began for me in 2003. I felt guided by spirit as I made my decision to give teaching a go and held my first psychic development group, with six people, on a Monday evening. We met once a week and each Sunday evening before the group, I would ask spirit what I should teach the group that coming Monday night. On most occasions I did not get my answer until a few hours before the group was about to start, but I trusted them and each week we had an interesting time with each other.

As the months passed I received requests from other people to join my group. Eventually the group became too large and also people were joining at different stages of their psychic journey, some with no knowledge at all. It was then that I decided to start another group and eventually the beginners group was born, which is what this book is based on. Over the years I have lost count of the number of people I have encouraged and helped with their spiritual growth, many of which sat with me for a great number of years and have become very good friends.

I have worked with spirit in many other ways such as doing private readings to help people connect to their loved ones who are in spirit or to guide them through obstacles in their life. I have also performed many psychic demonstrations to various audiences and led some spiritualist church services. At one time or another I have used all the tools in this book and it is through doing this I have been able to share my knowledge with you.

When I gave spirit the reins to lead me along my spiritual path, I trusted them completely and still do to this day. They have never let me down. In writing my book I want to share the things spirit and other people have taught me on my journey.

Please remember, as you read this book, that these are my thoughts and beliefs, which I have acquired along my spiritual path. I do not say that they are the only way or the correct way to do things. Other people may have their own ideas and even yourself. I do believe though, that there are no right or wrong ways to do things, as long as you are not hurting other people, so if it feels right for you then it is right. I am just giving you my thoughts and ideas that you can use, adapt to your own beliefs or ignore completely. I only ask that you stay true to yourself and your journey with spirit.

Let the fun begin.

Chapter Two
Lesson One - PROTECTION

Before we begin your psychic development journey, I first need to talk about protection.

Protecting yourself is very important when you start working with spirit. As on earth, with good and bad people, there are also good and bad spirits, who all want to connect in some way with you. As soon as you make the decision to start on this path, you become a beacon to spirit and they are very keen to make themselves known to you. When we are working with spirit, we want to work with the good guys and in love and light. So we say a little prayer of protection every time before we begin our work of any kind, including meditating, giving readings of every description, giving healing and contacting spirit in any way. You can say anything that feels right to you, with the intention being more important than the words. My starting prayer goes like this:

Spirit guides - I ask for love, light and protection around me at this time, of the highest and the best. Thank you for helping me grow on my spiritual path. Amen.

With a prayer you are protected from negativity, plus you are in control, and for me that is what I want to be. Spirit know when I am working with them as soon as I say my opening prayer, and after my closing prayer, they know we are finished. For the rest of the time they do not contact me unless it is really necessary, such as reminding me about something or keeping me away from danger. You may feel that you want spirit to contact you all the time but this can become draining and even a nuisance. The choice ultimately is yours but I prefer to choose when I work with spirit and it also keeps me in control and able to focus on my everyday life. If spirit were to contact you all the time, it could eventually become like that annoying friend who won't leave you alone. She is forever telling you something but she never listens to you. You feel depleted of positive energy and become irritated so much so that you cannot focus on anything. Unless this is what you really want, I would suggest you take control from the very start.

I always say please and thank you to spirit, as I would to a friend but if they start to annoy me, I tell them to go away! You will have a stronger connection and a stronger understanding of spirit if you build structure and create rules for you all to follow. You may not be able to see them but they will become your friends and a big part of your life.

I mentioned the bad spirits being around you. Please don't worry about this because, as long as you say a little prayer each time you start any psychic work, you will be protected. If at anytime you feel uncomfortable with the energy you are working with, tell spirit to go away and send love and light in their direction. If you still feel unsettled then cleanse the room you are working in by using a candle, smudging with some sage or by making a noise, and ask for any negativity to be taken away. I will talk about this more in chapter twelve, but for now just know that the intention is greater than trying to be perfect here.

When I end any session with spirit, I always say a closing prayer and give my thanks to spirit, just as I would to anyone who has worked with me or helped me. Again, please do not worry about being perfect with your words but to help you here is my closing prayer:

Spirit guides - thank you for working with me today. May you help me to live my life fully and keep growing my connection to the energy, love and light of those who trod this way before me. Amen.

This may feel strange and you may not feel that comfortable with saying a prayer but as time goes on, and the more you do this, it will become second nature and it will be something you won't need to think about. It will eventually feel natural and normal for you to do. Also make the words fit you. If you are not comfortable with saying amen you can just say thank you. There is no right or wrong way so just make it feel right for you and your beliefs.

Another thing I feel is important for me and enables me to get the best from spirit and myself, is to create a good, comfortable and peaceful working space. If you are lucky enough to have a spare room you can use in your house, that is great but if you are going to be using your everyday living area then just add a few things when you begin your work to create the perfect space for you to work in. I always light a candle before I start and, if I feel background music is necessary, I use soft relaxing music, which has no words and no significant tune that may attract my attention. I like the lighting to be low and incense sticks burning. These are my preferences but make your space to suit your needs. You may find you start one way and then alter it another time. Again there is no right or wrong way; whatever feels right for you is right.

DIFFERENT TYPES OF PROTECTION

Sometimes we need protection from people in our everyday life such as the kind of people who take our energy, who are always negative and who do not want to look on the positive side of things. After you have been in their presence you feel tired, sad, angry or cannot concentrate on anything except what they talked to you about. Think about your body language while they are around and, if you find yourself with arms crossed, body tense or just on edge, then it could help if you put yourself in some form of protection so that their negativity cannot attach to you.

There are a number of different ways to do this. Here are a few:-

Bubble - This, for me, is the easiest and fastest way of protection against negativity. There are a couple of ways to use this method. The first way is to put yourself inside a bubble, which then protects you from an individual person or a number of people who may be causing you unease. Just ask your guides to put a bubble around you.(I ask for a pink bubble but you can choose any colour that makes you feel happy). I usually say *"Spirit guides, please surround me with a pink bubble of love, light and protection while I am in this situation / with this person. Thank you."* Use any words that you feel comfortable with. You don't have to worry about remembering to pop the bubble as spirit will do that when you leave the situation.

It does not always have to be protection from individual people. Another reason for putting yourself inside a bubble is to protect yourself in stores where the lights are so bright and the crowds are too much to bear. For any situation you are in where you feel uncomfortable or drained after being there for a while, use the bubble technique.

You can also put the other person into a bubble. For example, if you are in a room full of people and one person is being annoying to many other people, put that person into the bubble. This then protects everyone in the room and it is quite fascinating to watch the change of energy in the room when this is done.

Dome - This is very similar to the bubble technique but a dome is a solid object for situations that are a bit more intense. I very rarely put a dome over myself as I don't like the feeling of being restricted, but it is extremely useful to use over very negative people.

Suit of armour - You could use this when situations become even more negative around you. Use it over yourself in the same way as the bubble technique.

Wall - Use this method when you need to be divided from a situation where other techniques would not protect you enough. Using a wall is a complete divide where virtually nothing is able to get through.

When using any of these suggestions, and others that you may think about, have a set of words to use that feel right for you. Assess the situation and use the appropriate tool suitable for that moment in time. I mainly use the bubble as I feel it is not too overwhelming. The over use of the other techniques, especially around ourselves, could start to separate us from people. Although protection is very good at times, we should also try and work with our own ability to not allow other peoples energies and auras to affect us.

PROTECTION EXERCISES

1   Write your start and finish prayer. Use words that feel natural for you to say. Try to add the words love, light and protection into your prayer, as long as you feel comfortable with them. If they don't feel right for you try and find alternatives. Using these words does keep you protected from the dark or negative side of the spirit world.

2   Create the right atmosphere, which will allow you to work in peace and relaxation. Nothing is set in stone and you can always change or add things at any time, until you find what works for you.

3 Sit comfortably in your special space. Say your opening prayer, then sit quietly and feel relaxed in the moment. When you feel the time is right you can say your closing prayer. Make any notes of anything you felt, sensed or relevant thoughts that came to mind during that time.

4   Place yourself in a bubble of protection against a situation or person. Make notes on what you said and how the situation was different from when you didn't use a bubble.

5   At an appropriate time try and use one of the other protection techniques making notes on the whole process.

notes

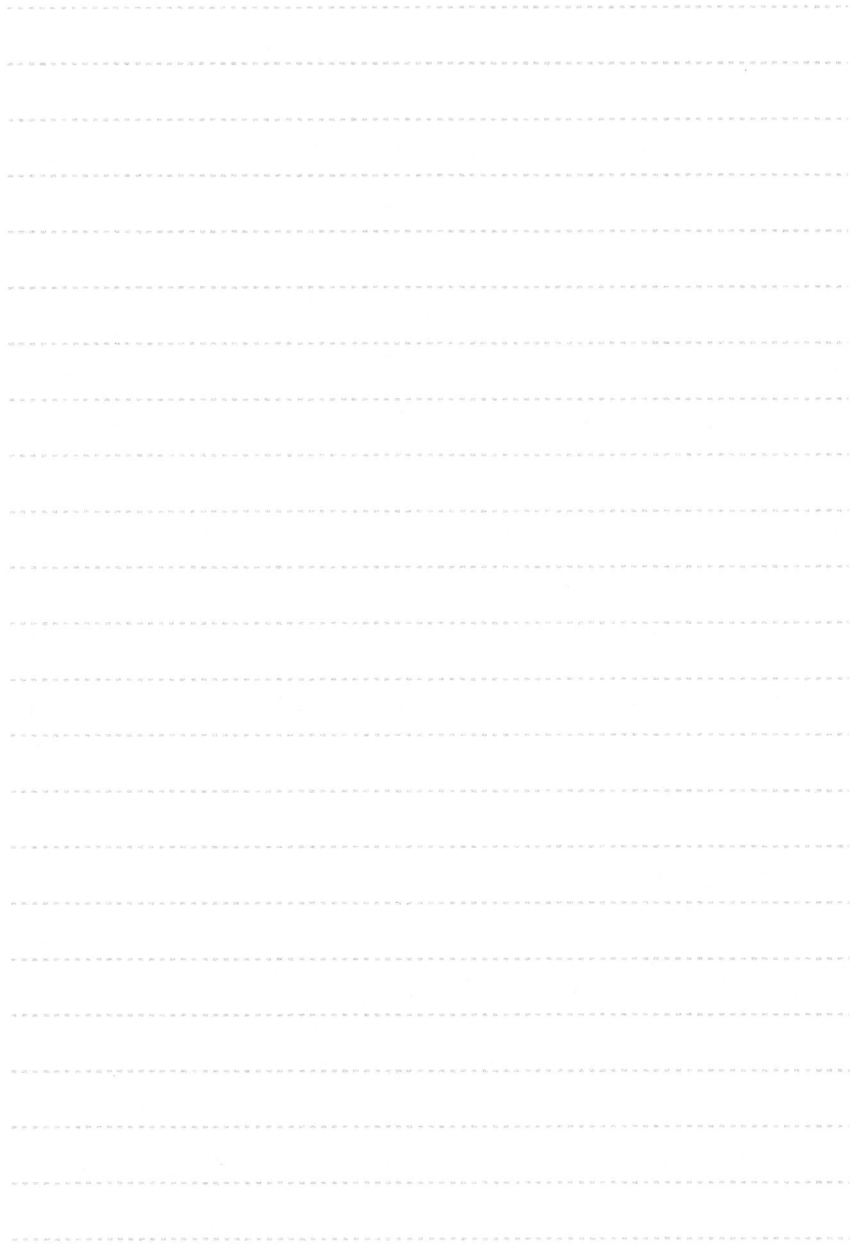

Chapter Three
Lesson Two - FEELING SPIRIT

Some people are very excited to begin their psychic journey and others can be a little unsure, but are intrigued to know more. I believe everyone has the ability to develop any psychic skill even if some people are more aware than others, but everyone can learn. Psychic development is similar to learning how to drive a car; you know all the pedals do something and before your first lesson you may even already know what each one does, but somebody teaches you and eventually you can drive on your own without instruction. This is what I do with psychic development; you already have the tools within you, I just show you how to bring them out and use them. For some people the journey is easy, for others, things may take a little longer but however it is for you, know that you are capable. If you believe in yourself and trust in spirit, the goal of being on platform or whatever you hope to achieve, will be the end result.

So let us begin your psychic development journey.

I always start people the same way no matter what they may or may not know. Try to relax because trying too hard can cause things to take longer to develop. Build that trust in yourself and believe and know that when you are working with spirit your thoughts, feelings and emotions are spirit connecting with you. Trust and know that spirit want to work with you and, if you allow this to happen, you will develop a great skill with them.

Spirit is around you all the time. Some people may already know this, or sense this, while others just need to accept the fact. For those of you who need some help recognising when spirit are around, here are some ways they can make contact with you. You should recognise that one or two of these may have already happened to you.

* It can feel as if you have walked into a cobweb, across your face, but there is nothing there.
* It can feel as if someone is playing with your hair but there is no-one there.
* You feel a coldness around you or an area of your body goes cold, but where you are is warm.
* You sense there is someone in the room with you but you are alone.
* You saw someone out of the corner of your eye but there is no one there.
* You hear someone call your name but you are alone.

* An object moves or falls for no apparent reason but there is no one near it.
And many more.

These are all ways spirit is trying to get your attention. Think about the occasions when some or all of these things have happened to you. What were you doing? Were you thinking of a loved one who has passed over or were you in a difficult situation where you needed guidance? Perhaps in your mind you were asking for help because you were thinking about how to change a pattern or path in your life? Or maybe you were joyful and thinking how lucky you were.

If you don't recall anything like this happening to you, but you would like something to, now is the time to pay more attention to your own body. This is something I feel is very important with psychic growth because, if you know how your body feels in every way then you will know when spirit is trying to connect with you. Watch out for these signs and maybe you can add a few more to the list above.

When you are ready to invite spirit to work with you it is a good idea to know yourself first. Remember, always know how your body feels then you will know when spirit is touching you. Spirit guides and your loved ones who are in spirit, contact you in different ways so that you can eventually know who is who. Keep notes on the different ways spirit touch you and then, if the same thing keeps happening, you can ask who they are. The answer will be a thought in your head or just a knowing that it is a certain someone, and it is normally the first person you think of in that moment. If you should be wrong, spirit will let you know but this is a good way to start so trust and believe this.

Many people experience trouble accepting that spirit communicate in this way and question their thoughts as being their own and not spirit answering them. Only a small percentage of people actually hear spirit talk to them. The more you practice communicating with spirit the more you will trust and believe that in the moment you are working with them your thoughts and knowings are to do with the messages they are sending you.

FEELING SPIRIT EXERCISES

1   Think of all the ways spirit has contacted you. Write them down and over the next few days be aware of other ways they are trying to connect with you and add them to your list. Acknowledge spirit when you feel them. You could say something like "Thank you, I am aware of you around me, please connect with me more often." The more you respond to them the more they will contact you and want to work with you. If you keep ignoring them they will go away.

2   Sit in your special place and say your opening prayer. Scan your body and notice how it feels - any aches or pains, are you warm or cold, are you tired, happy, sad? When you are ready, ask spirit to move close to you and to give you some sign that they are around. Anything that happens, any feelings, sensations, pains or emotions at this time will be from spirit. Acknowledge their presence and then ask spirit to step away. Whatever you were experiencing should stop. When you are ready repeat the process. Working with this exercise will help you become more sensitive to spirit and eventually you will feel them without even trying. When you are ready you can say your closing prayer.

3   Repeat the above exercise but this time ask a loved one who you have in spirit to move close to you. Make a

mental note of what you are experiencing with them, and then ask that they step away from you. Repeat this a few times. Your loved one should touch you in the same way each time. This will be their sign to you so that you will know when they are around. Make a note of what happened and then repeat with other loved ones.

4   Repeat the same exercise but this time ask one of your guides to move close to you. Use the same principle of finding out how they will let you know when they are around you. When you are happy with that, ask your guide his or her name, which area of your psychic work he or she is going to work with you and anything else you would like to know such as their age, where they are from, how they died, etc. The answer to any question will be the first thing that pops into your head or just a knowing. Don't question it, just accept it and make a note of all you have discovered.

5   When you feel confident enough you can ask a friend if you can bring one of their loved ones through for them. Ask spirit questions to build up a picture of the person. When you have gathered all the information, tell your friend all you have learnt about their loved one and ask them for feedback.

If you are struggling with any of these exercises, please do not be disheartened. Keep trying and believe you can do this. Sometimes we can try too hard or expect too much but if we relax and trust ourselves we will always achieve our goal. Also remember that spirit is probably not going to appear in front of you as a human form. Most of the time, they will be a thought in your head or a knowing in your heart. It is very important, therefore, to always be aware of what is going on, in and around your body, before you begin work, in order to gain the correct information from spirit. Remember that practice, belief and trust will eventually get you the results that you are looking for.

notes

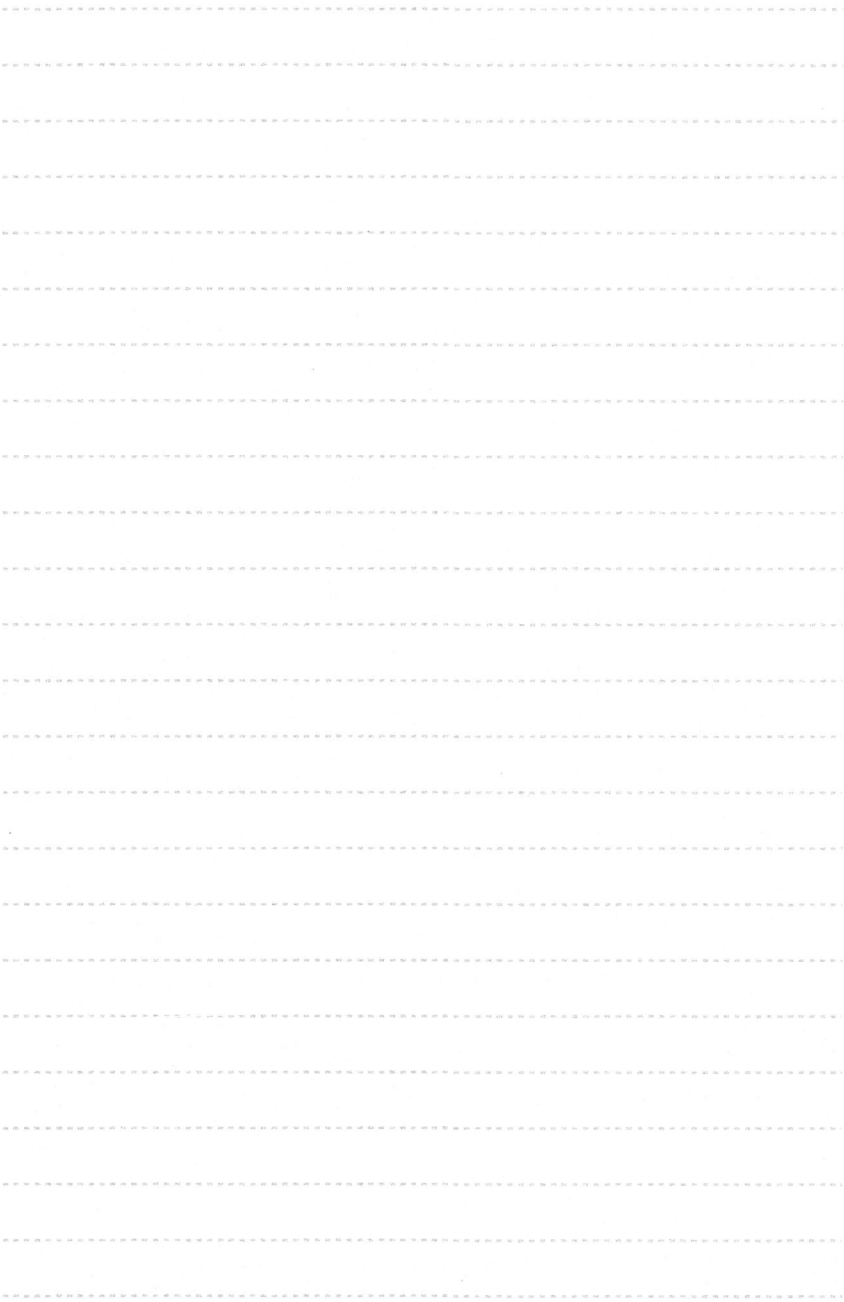

Chapter Four
Lesson Three - **MEDITATION**

Meditation is a non-starter for many people for all sorts of reasons, but the main one being because they think they have to totally empty their minds. I don't believe this to be true because we are human beings and our minds are always working and processing thoughts. When we think we have to stop thinking, we then start thinking that we can't stop thinking and that is the moment some feel they cannot meditate.

Sometimes we set ourselves too big of a goal and most of the time that is why we don't succeed. If we set ourselves small, realistic goals, in any area of our lives, we are more likely to achieve them and that then gives us the incentive to set more small and reachable goals. So with meditation, instead of trying to meditate for twenty minutes each day, set a goal of one minute a day which is very achievable. Eventually that one minute turns into two minutes, two minutes into three minutes and before we realise it the twenty minute goal has been reached.

WHY MEDITATE:

Meditation is an ancient practice, which offers tremendous benefits and does not require any specific beliefs or special talents. We only need our self, our mind and a few minutes where we will not be disturbed.

Meditation helps to quiet the mind from our everyday thinking and brings focus to our intuitive, subconscious mind.

Meditation brings peace and calm into our lives which allows us to be in touch with our bodies, which in turn helps us to know when spirit is trying to communicate with us.

Meditation raises our body's vibration so that the gap between spirit and our self becomes smaller. Spirit's energy vibrates at a higher frequency than ours, therefore the more we meditate the higher our vibration becomes and the more messages we should receive.

Meditation helps us contact our higher self easier, as our thoughts and ideas are coming from deep within our mind at this time.

Meditation is also a direct link to our inner-self so we can do some self-healing during meditation, especially when using affirmations during the meditation.

Meditation allows spirit to communicate with us, giving answers and guidance as we open up to them during this relaxed state.

HOW TO MEDITATE

1 Prepare your room as you would for any work with spirit - light a candle, you could either have silence or some soft music playing which has no meaning to you, have low lights or just use the candle light. Try different things and eventually get a routine that creates a comfortable place for your meditations.

2   Remember to turn all phones off or disconnect them before you start, as any sudden noises when you are in deep meditation can bring you back with a jolt and doesn't make you feel too good.

3 I suggest you meditate sitting up, either on a chair or on the floor, so you can stay awake and be aware of what is happening during your meditation.

4   Place your hands on your lap with palms facing up, which signifies you are ready to receive information.

5   Say your opening prayer.

6 Close your eyes and take a deep breath in through your nose, hold for a few seconds and release it out through your nose. Repeat this two more times and each time feel your body relaxing a little more. Now bring your breathing back to normal, taking nice steady breaths through your nose.

7   Concentrate on breathing in and out. If your mind wanders just allow the thoughts to come in and then send them on their way and bring your attention back to your breath.

8   Sit like this for as long as you feel comfortable. There is no time limit but each time you practice the longer you will want to sit.

9   When you feel the time is right to stop, bring yourself back to focusing on the noises around you. Take a few deep breaths then wiggle your fingers and toes and open your eyes.

10 Say your closing prayer and, when you are ready, write down the length of time you meditated and any thoughts or things which happened during that time.

If you are struggling with meditation you could use something as a visual focus such as a candle. Place this in front of you and each time you feel your mind wandering, acknowledge it, let it go and then bring your attention back to the candle.

Another way to meditate is by using a guided meditation that will help to keep you focused. The person reading them normally starts with an opening prayer and finishes with a closing prayer, although it would not hurt to do your own prayer as well. Guided meditations last for different lengths of times and normally have moments for you to connect with your guides or whatever they have led you to envisage.

When you are beginning with meditation try all the different ways and see which works best for you. You may find different ones are needed at different times, depending on the result you are looking for. Any kind of meditation will benefit you in your psychic growth.

Things to remember

It takes time, perseverance and repetition to learn meditation.

Meditating everyday is more important than the length of time you practice every day.

Every meditation will be different, so keep a journal and make notes about each one - time of day, length of time you meditated, music used if any, what happened during the meditation such as your thoughts, visitors and how you felt before and after.

Remember - little steps lead to big steps.

MEDITATION EXERCISES

1   Set a time everyday for a week to do a one minute meditation. Make notes each time and allow your progress to grow.

2   On the second week each time you meditate, ask a question and listen for the answer. Write down your question and the response you received each time.

3 Try different kinds of meditation and keep a note of how they benefit you.

4   Get to know your spirit guides during meditation. Ask them questions about themselves and how they will connect with you.

5   Meditate with a set of goals you are trying to achieve in your mind and ask for some clear guidance during the meditation. Remember to make notes for future reference.

notes

Chapter Five
Lesson Four - **PENDULUM**

A pendulum is a weight hung mostly from a chain or cord so that it can swing freely in any direction. The weight can be a crystal, a stone, a charm or just about anything which is not too light.

Using a pendulum is a great visual for answers to questions. It is another tool that you can use to communicate with your guides, helpers or higher self. Pendulums can be very accurate if you use them correctly and are best suited to questions that require a yes or no answer. A pendulum works by reacting to your subconscious mind, the part we don't normally communicate with very well. It acts as a receiver and transmitter of information from your spirit helpers. You can use anything as a pendulum, it just needs to swing. I own a few pendulums and use each one for different purposes, but that is my preference. I have crystal pendulums and metal pendulums but a necklace can work just as well.

When choosing a pendulum to buy always try them first. Some pendulums may not want to work with you - strange but true! The people who sell pendulums will expect you to try them for this very reason. Before you make your choice, think about what you are going to use the pendulum for and then choose one you are drawn to. When you get a new pendulum cleanse it before you use it and, if it is going to be used for one purpose only, such as healing, you can dedicate it for that too.

Carry the pendulum with you as you get to know it; this will allow for better connection between you as you work with it. Use it everyday and keep notes on the questions you have asked and the answers it has given you. This will not only build your connection with your pendulum but will also build your confidence and trust with it.

Remember to cleanse your pendulum, preferably after each use.

HOW TO USE A PENDULUM

As with all things you do with spirit, especially when learning something new, you need to relax, trust and don't try too hard.

1 Hold the chain of the pendulum about 1-2 inches above the crystal, or whatever you have hanging on the end of

the chain, with the excess chain curled in your palm. Your grip needs to be relaxed and the chain should be held between your thumb and index finger so that the pendulum can swing in any direction without hindrance from your other fingers or hand.

2   While sitting on a chair, lean forward slightly and rest the arm holding the pendulum on your leg with that same wrist resting in your other hand. The pendulum should be able to move with nothing in its way whilst your arm and hand are being supported to help prevent them from moving. As you become more competent and trusting towards your pendulum you may not need this support.

3   Now in your mind, or out loud, ask the pendulum to show you its *yes* swing. It may take a little time for the pendulum to move but don't worry, just keep running the question over and over. Eventually the pendulum should begin to move. It could swing in a circle going either clockwise or anticlockwise, backwards, forwards or side-to-side. Whichever way it moves for you make a note of this. When you are happy that you have the reply for your *yes* swing, ask the pendulum to show you its *no* swing and lastly ask for its *maybe* swing.

My *yes* swing is a side-to-side movement, my *no* swing is backwards and forwards, and my *maybe* swing is in a circle. There is no right or wrong way for your pendulum to swing, so don't try to make it do something different than its natural swing. Sometimes my pendulum will not answer a question and just stays completely still. I know that this means I have to live my life and wait for that particular thing to happen - I can sometimes be too nosey and impatient!

WAYS TO USE A PENDULUM

Ask questions about a job, new house, relationships, travel, just about anything.

Finding lost objects. For example, if your pendulum has indicated that the object is in your home, you could either walk into each room and ask your pendulum if it is there or stay where you are and say the name of the room and ask if it is there. When you know the actual room the object is in, you can walk around that room using the pendulum to find the exact location of it.

Learn if the food you eat is good for your body by either holding the pendulum over the food and asking or by naming the food and asking.

Checking your chakras which is explained in chapter thirteen.

Making a choice between the same kind of things. For example, there are three cars you like but which one should you buy? Hold the pendulum over each picture and your yes swing will give you the answer.

To help you to make a decision. For example, you want to move house, you know the area (such as a ten mile radius) but you cannot decide the exact location. Get a map, circle the area and hold your pendulum over it until it shows you the answer.

MY ROUTINE

As with every task I do with spirit, I have a routine that I use. There is no right or wrong way with this because it should just be what feels right for you and what works for you. Here's my routine.

After saying my opening prayer, I hold the pendulum in my hands and I cleanse it with my breathe. (More on the different ways of cleansing in Chapter Twelve)

I close my eyes and take a couple of deep breathes to help relax and centre myself.

I pull the blue light I see in my minds eye from above the top of my head down through my body into the earth and then back out of the ground up through my body.

I ask the pendulum (spirit) if it will work with me for questions about whatever the subject is at that time. If it gives me a yes swing I then start to ask my questions. If it gives me a no swing I thank it and put it back into its pouch. Remember, spirit know what we are going to be asking questions about before we have a conscious thought about it. Sometimes, as human beings, we want to know answers to things that really we have no business to know about, such as a friend's relationship. It is times like this that spirit denies access to these answers. You could still go ahead and ask your questions but remember the answers will probably not be correct.

If I have more questions, but on a different subject, I ask the pendulum again if it will work with me on the new matter. The reason for doing this at the start of every new subject is so I know the answers spirit will give me will be correct, as I have had permission to ask the questions on that particular topic.

When I have finished asking my questions I say thank you, I cleanse the pendulum again with my breathe and place it in its pouch ready for the next time, and finish with my closing prayer.

This may sound very long and complicated but it works for me, and really only takes a few seconds to complete.   It has become a natural thing for me to do, so much so that I don't need to think about it any more, I just do it!

THINGS TO REMEMBER:

Always try a pendulum before you buy it as some may not want to work with you. Whoever is selling pendulums will always expect you to try before you buy.

Whenever you use a new pendulum always check your yes, no and maybe swings. Do not ever assume all pendulums will use the same swings. They can and do vary.

A quivering pendulum means it has a great connection with you.

A small swing or movement can mean that there is some doubt. A really strong, fast, positive swing means a definite yes, or no, and it could be happening almost immediately.

Always have your feet on the ground when asking questions with your pendulum as this keeps you grounded and focused. Lying on the bed can give false answers.

Check with your pendulum that you may ask about each subject, as some questions may not be appropriate for you to know the answers. For example, asking about your friend's marriage without asking permission from your friend to do this, is not appropriate and really none of your business. If the answer is yes you may proceed if the answer is no then believe you will not receive the correct reply even if you should still go ahead with asking the question.

Do not keep asking the same question. The pendulum is like your friend. In both cases, if you do not listen to their replies to your questions and keep asking the same thing over and over again, eventually they will just say what you want to hear which is not necessarily the truth.

Make sure your questions are specific and exact. For example, if you want to have a dessert after dinner and you ask your pendulum "Is it good to have dessert?" that is not clear as it could mean everyday you want dessert. So instead ask "Is it good for me to have dessert now?"

Another example is if you are about to go on a car journey to Scotland and you ask your pendulum "Does my car need fuel?" Your pendulum will answer yes because the car needs fuel to operate all the time. Instead ask "Do I have enough fuel in my car to get me to Scotland?" Also remember that if someone has told you a tale about another person and you ask the pendulum if the tale is true, you may not get a correct answer as some of the tale may be true and some may be false, so ask about certain situations in the tale.

If you try to influence the pendulum it will give you the answer you want, and this may not be true.

Although your pendulum can answer all your questions, you should not rely on it for everything in your daily life. Make your own decisions with and without using your pendulum and find a happy balance.

PENDULUM EXERCISES

1 Think about a beginning and ending routine which feels comfortable and works for you. Practice this routine until it feels natural. You may need to change it a few times but when you feel happy with it write it down and use this every time you use your pendulum.

2 Find your yes, no and maybe swings. Write these down and then ask a question that you know the answer too. Ask one with a yes answer and one with a no answer. For example I could ask for my yes answer, is my name Jacqueline? For my no answer I could ask, am I a boy ?

3 Think of a subject you would like some guidance with and ask your pendulum if it will work with you. If it replies yes continue with asking some questions. Keep a note of the questions and answers you receive so that you can check back later when it has happened. If it says no then think of another subject.

4 Experiment with the foods you eat by asking your pendulum if each item is good for you. When you receive a no answer, stop there and don't eat that food for a week and see how you feel.

5 Ask someone to hide something in the house and use your pendulum to find it.

6 To receive more detailed answers to questions, draw a large circle on a piece of paper and divide it into 26 segments. Write a letter of the alphabet in each segment. Use this circle to allow your pendulum to spell out words when asking questions. Hold your pendulum about two inches over the centre of the circle and ask your question. Make notes of your questions and answers given.

notes

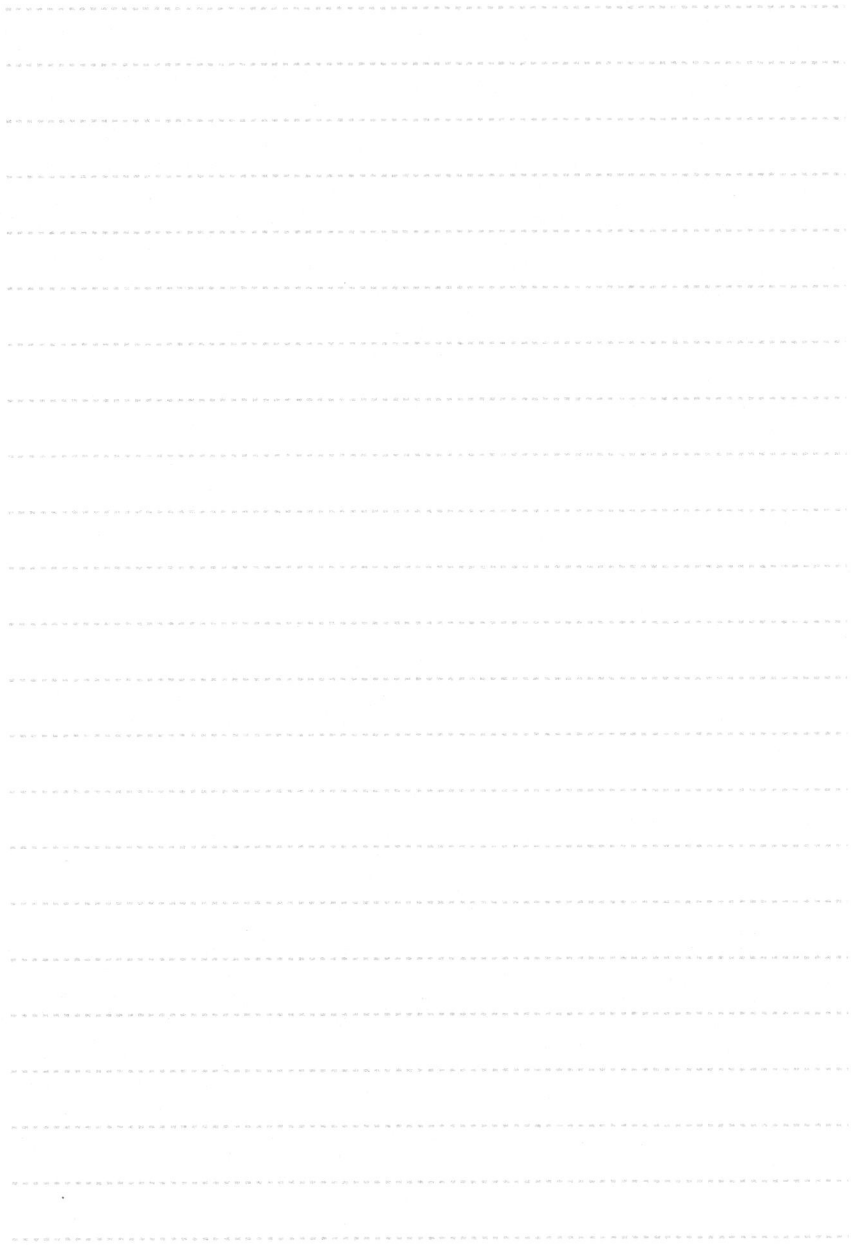

Chapter Six
Lesson Five - AURAS

An aura is the energy field around any living thing - a human, an animal, a living plant and even trees. Auras tend to look like a halo or a glow and sometimes you may see colours and even objects in them.

Not everyone is aware of their aura, but think about when you meet someone for the first time. With some people you can feel all prickly and not very comfortable in their presence and with others you may feel warm and completely comfortable, almost as if you have met them before. This is your aura touching their aura and, before you have had time to think about the person in any detail, your aura has already assessed them as either being a friend or foe for you. If you haven't noticed this happening before, then the next time you meet someone new, check out your immediate reaction to him or her - I have never found my auras message to be wrong.

Your aura is also at work when you walk into a room filled with people. Straight away it gives you a sense of the atmosphere in the room. You will either feel comfortable or you will sense tension. This is your aura assessing the energies for you.

Another example of your aura helping you is when you are alone in a room and, without hearing a sound you get the sense that someone has walked in. Again your aura is warning you and preparing you for visitors, be they friend or foe.

Your aura is also at work to let you know when spirit is around. When spirit move close to you, you first feel them in your aura. This can be a gentle pressure, a change in temperature, a tiny flutter, a feeling that someone has wrapped their arms around you or any sensation that changes how your outer body feels.

When you are in tune with your body, you are also in tune with your aura and having this awareness will help you in your everyday activities. Trusting the messages your aura gives you will help you to make quick and accurate decisions about people and situations you find yourself in.

Your aura is your protection and changes along with your mood or the environment you are in. If you are in the presence of people you don't feel comfortable with, your aura will shrink around you, almost like creating a strong shield to protect you. When you are happy and in an environment with people you feel at ease with, your aura will expand, welcoming people into your space. This explains why people feel drawn to us and want to be near us when we are happy and smiley with a magnetic air about us. The reverse is true when we feel nervous, cold and almost hostile to other people. No one wants to come near us. Watch out for this when you are around different people.

Being able to see auras can be used on its own to give someone a reading or used in conjunction with other tools. Our auras change as our moods and thoughts change, so having this skill helps when giving any kind of reading.

Seeing auras can be an easy, natural thing for some people to do but for others they may struggle with it or even never be able to do it. If this is something you have difficulty mastering, you can use your minds eye to see auras, with a sense of knowing what it looks like. Either way is fine. Trying too hard to see auras just leads to frustration and a belief it will never happen. If you use your sense of knowing and build on that, one day you should actually see them because you will become more relaxed with learning this ability.

Only look at someone's aura if you have his or her permission. Being able to see auras is a gift that should not be abused. My feelings are, if you look at someone's aura without them knowing, it is the same as looking inside someone's bag without their permission. When people know you can see auras they can feel intimidated by you and even a little worried at what you can see. Letting them know you need their permission first before you take a look, can help to put them at ease. Also if people are wary of your ability they can, without realising it, shrink their aura thus making a true reading almost impossible. Keeping people relaxed is key to giving a positive reading.

HOW TO SEE AURAS

If you don't already see auras, here is a good way to begin. Hold your hand out in front of you and look at your aura. It may, at first, look like a glow around the outside of your hand. If you are having trouble seeing it, try to look with lazy eyes, almost cross-eyed. You need to look to the side of your hand rather than straight at it. For any of you who remember The Magic Eye books, around in the 1990's, the same principle for looking at those works for seeing auras. If it doesn't happen straight away, keep trying but don't get frustrated by it. Try again later or another day.

Eventually, the more you practice this, you should start to see colours and sometimes even shapes or items in auras. These all add to the reading. Whatever you see, give the meaning that comes into your mind as you see the colour, shape or item. Don't think about it because then your logical mind will come into play and you will try to make sense of it, which will then lead you to give your version of the reading rather than offering what spirit want you to give.

COLOUR MEANINGS

Here is a list of some colour meanings, although using your intuition with the colours you see will be more accurate for each reading, especially as the meaning of colours can vary depending on circumstances and how the energy of the individual is in that moment. Also each colour can have many different shades and this can alter the interpretation. For example, a dark red could mean passion and romance whereas a bright red could mean danger. Remember, it's the interpretation in the moment which is correct for that person, as seeing the same colour in a different reading could give a different interpretation. Each colour can also have a negative or a positive meaning - again interpret the colour in the moment for an exact reading.

Black - death, evil, mystery, protection, dramatic, elegance, formality, sophistication, sensuality, power, bold, strength

Blue - coldness, fear, tranquility, loyalty, security, trust, intelligence, peace, stability, calmness, confidence, sincerity, affection, integrity, faith, wisdom, truth, friendship

Brown - dogmatic, conservative, friendly, earth, outdoors, longevity, homeliness, concentration, courage, energy

Green - envy, jealousy, guilt, money, growth, harmony, fertility, vitality, freshness, healing, balance, life, environment, safety, relaxation, stability, endurance, peace, soothing, natural

Orange - ignorance, sluggishness, thirst, courage, confidence, friendliness, success, adventure, creativity, excitement, wisdom, wealth, attraction, youthful, happiness

Pink - weak, immaturity, femininity, sensitivity, emotional, healthy, happiness, compassion, sweet, playful, romance, faithfulness, beauty, friendship, appreciation, gratitude, admiration, unconditional love, tenderness

Purple - mysterious, moodiness, arrogant, sadness, royalty, nobility, spirituality, power, luxury, ambition, wisdom, passion, vision, magic, dignity, creativity

Red - energy, danger, strength, power, determination, spontaneity, passion, romance, desire, love

White - coolness, goodness, innocence, purity, freshness, easy, cleanliness, hope, light, simplicity, truth, protection, healing

Yellow - irresponsible, unstable, caution, cowardice, childish, bright, energy, creativity, intellect, happiness, joy, cheerfulness, friendliness, warmth, freshness, optimism

SEEING OBJECTS IN THE AURA

When you see objects in an aura, think what they mean to you and your interpretation of them in that moment. For example, seeing a pencil could mean the person needs to write; seeing vegetables could mean the person needs to check their diet; seeing a plane could mean the person will travel over seas. Always go with your first thought or instinct and trust this to be correct. Do not stop and think about it, as your logical mind will come into play. If something comes to mind and you feel it doesn't make sense or you don't understand it, just give the message - it is not yours to understand or to decide if the person needs to hear it or not. If you don't deliver the messages spirit is giving you, they will eventually stop giving them to you. You are simply the messenger and the person you are reading for has to make sense of the reading not you.

The more you can practice aura readings the easier and better you will get. If you have a pet, you can practice looking at their aura.

AURA READING EXERCISES

1 Start becoming aware of your aura and the way you feel when you meet someone new. Notice how your aura changes when you feel different emotions and are in different environments.

2 The next time you walk into a room full of people, get a sense of the energies in the room as soon as you walk through the door. Make a mental note of what you are sensing before talking to anyone and see if you are correct.

3 Ask spirit to move close to you and feel your aura change.

4 Hold your hands out in-front of you with your palms facing each other about 12 inches apart. Very slowly start to move your palms together, paying attention to what you can feel. This may take a few tries but eventually you should start to feel energy between your palms. The closer you push your palms together the stronger this energy should become. This is your aura around your hands meeting. You can bounce your palms together and really feel your aura. The slower you do this, especially when you first start doing this, the easier it will be to feel your aura.

70

5 Hold your hand out in-front of you and look at your aura around it. Think a sad thought and watch your aura change. Think a happy thought and see the change again.

6 Ask someone to sit or stand in front of you so you can read their aura. Work out the meaning of the colours, shapes or items you see or sense. Get feedback from them to see if your messages are correct.

notes

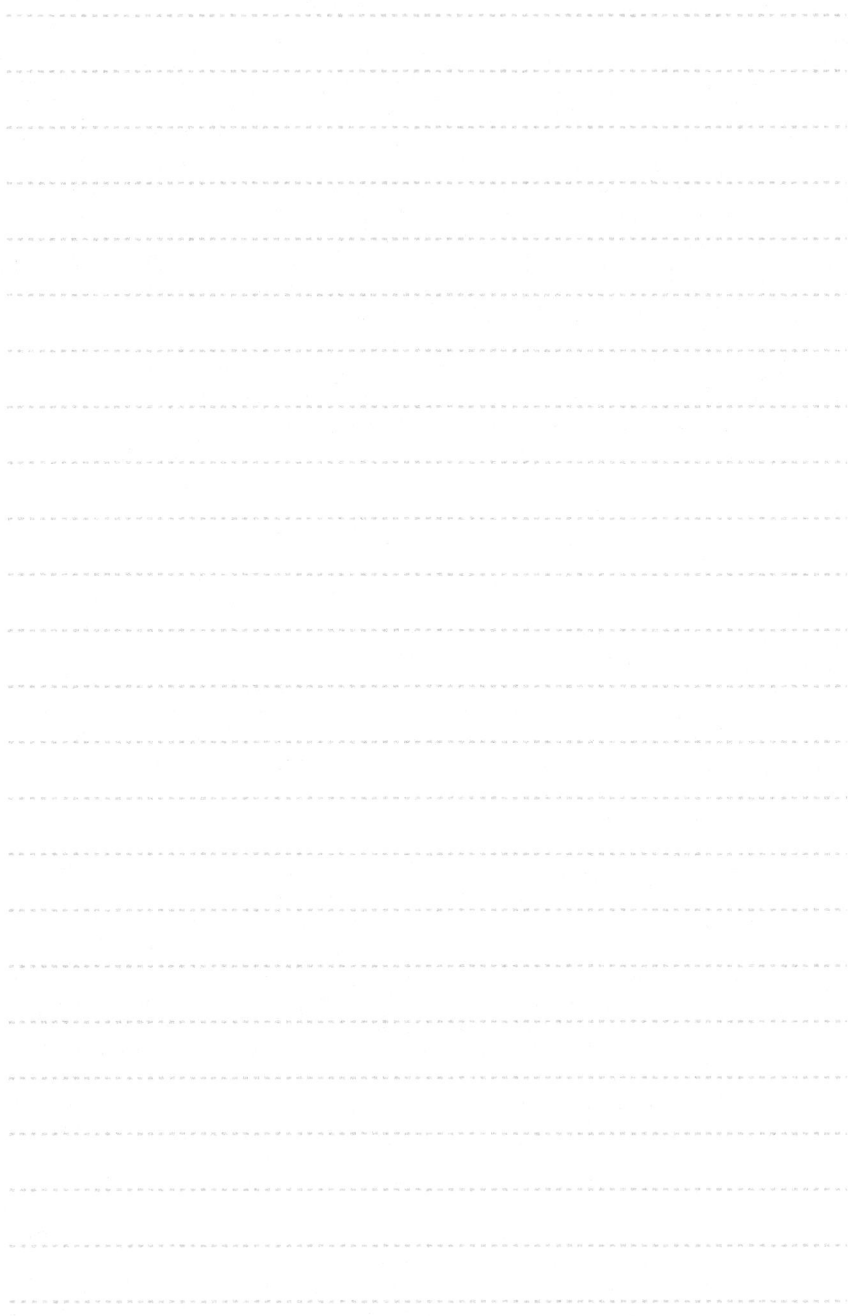

CHAPTER SEVEN
Lesson Six - **PSYCHOMETRY**

Psychometry is the ability to read objects and get a sense of the history behind them and the people they belonged to. While holding them you may also receive messages in the form of images, sounds, smells, tastes and even emotions.

When trying to communicate with someone who has passed, it is sometimes easier to make a connection if you can hold something that once belonged to him or her. The item should still contain information about its previous owner, like a psychic imprint. Their energies should still be connected to the object, making connection easier, plus it helps to draw that person forward, almost like a calling card. You may be able to sense what the person looked like, what they did in life, how they were emotionally and even how they died.

Any object can be used - jewellery, a watch, a wallet, keys, photograph, an ornament they were fond of, literally anything. Preferably the object should have been in their possession for a long time, making the imprint good and strong. Even by standing next to a piece of furniture which belonged to them, or in a building by touching the walls, you can get a reading from this.

HOW TO PERFORM PSYCHOMETRY

1 Create the right environment and say your opening prayer. Now centre yourself and be aware of how your body feels before you begin.

2 Connect with your guides and ask spirit to move closer to assist with the reading.

3 Now, hold the object in your hand and close your eyes. Think about the item and make a connection with it, concentrating only on the object and how it is feeling in your hand.

4 Begin to ask some questions such as:-

How does the item feel?

How do I feel while holding the item?

What is going on with my body?

What thoughts are coming to mind?

5 Thank spirit and your guides for working with you and say your closing prayer.

Here is an example of a reading -

I am holding a ring with 3 stones set at the top, belonging to a female.

How does the item feel?

The stones feel rough as I run my fingers over them, therefore there could be a bit of tension around the owner of the ring. This tension could involve 3 people, or she could be stuck in the middle of tension between 2 other people who, I sense, are members of her family.

How do I feel while holding the item?

I feel extremely sad, agitated and bewildered. Although it doesn't feel like a recent passing, the situation still feels fresh so obviously something that the spirit still feels concerned by.

What is going on with my body?

I have the feeling of heartache and breathlessness plus my throat chakra seems blocked.

What thoughts are coming to mind?

I feel conversation could have been better and things discussed more. Certain things feel left unsaid .

Remember when you are giving a reading using any tool, how your body feels, your thoughts and emotions are not yours but are connected with the person you are doing the reading for or, in this case, the owner of the ring.

Feedback from the example reading -

The lady, who the ring belonged to, had passed a number of years ago. At the time, a family dispute between her two daughters was going on. She could understand both sides of the argument but felt unable to choose one daughter over the other and so felt stuck in the middle.   She was unsure of how to make this better or what to say to either of them and felt extremely heartbroken. She passed away after a really bad asthma attack with the situation still unresolved.

When you first start to give readings using psychometry, your messages may seem short, but with practice they will get longer.   Personal items hold so much information about their owner that the questions you can ask are endless; you just need to be curious enough to ask them.

PSYCHOMETRY EXERCISES

1 With your eyes closed, get someone to place something in your hand which you haven't seen before. Keeping your eyes closed throughout, give the reading of the object by trying to get a sense of who it belonged to, etc. Say whatever you see in your mind's eye, hear, feel or sense, without trying to process the information. Get the person with you to write everything down so you can discuss it after.

2 Hold an object which you have not seen before, that belonged to a distant relative who you don't know much about, but someone else in your family does. Give the reading of the object and then check your accuracy

3 Visit an historic house or an old building you do not know anything about. Walk around touching the walls and connecting to the building while interpreting the feelings in your body and mind. Write things down as you go around. At the end, read the tour guide leaflet or research the building to find out how accurate you have been.

4   Ask friends to share objects with you which belonged to their loved ones. Give them a reading and ask for feedback. Do this as often as you can to build your confidence and ability.

5   Try reading different objects and keep a note of each one.   This way you will discover which objects work better and faster for you, or you may find that working with any object gives a good connection.

notes

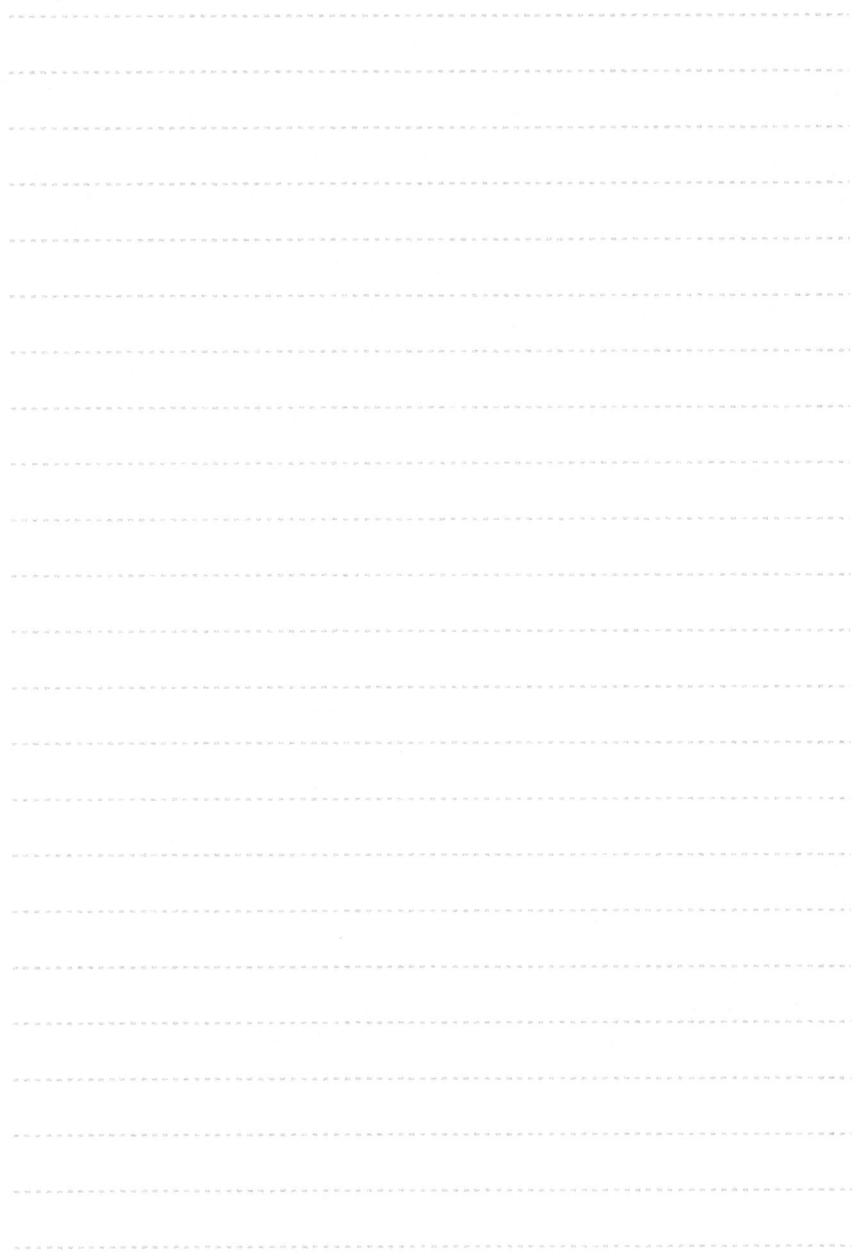

CHAPTER EIGHT
Lesson Seven - **CARDS**

In this chapter I am referring to Oracle cards.

There are Tarot cards and Oracle cards, both have many different designs for you to indulge in. I am going to talk about Oracle cards here, although the same principles apply to Tarot cards, and any other kinds of cards. All of the cards will give you wisdom, insight and advice for any question you may ask.

I feel you can never have enough cards and my collection is vast. There are so many different designs and topics, for example, unicorns, fairies, angels, crystals, flowers, animals, and also various shapes and sizes to choose from. When giving yourself, or others, a reading with cards it is always good to have different choices available, especially as the cards have different meanings to people for different subjects, different moods and different days.

Most packs of Oracle cards come with a little book that has an explanation to the meaning of each card. While these books are interesting, my feelings are to leave the book in the box and use your instinct and spirit's guidance to read the cards. The book is someone else's interpretation of the cards and, if we learn the book, each reading will become stilted, robotic and not at all natural. Also, we would not discover our own interpretation of the cards or connect with spirit, our feelings and emotions, as there would be no need to do so. Each card has a different message to tell depending on the question being asked. By building your own connection with your cards, you will eventually get a pattern and the underlying meaning of each individual card with the added ability of delivering a full reading with the help of spirit and your psychic abilities.

When choosing a new set of cards, find a shop where they have a demonstration deck which you can look at and hold. Most new packs of cards will be sealed and therefore you cannot tell if they would be right to work with. With a demonstration pack you can hold the cards and spend a little time seeing which ones you feel drawn to. You need to have a connection with your cards otherwise the readings won't happen or may not flow freely and easily. If you are buying your first set and feel overwhelmed with the choices available, start by choosing a subject which you enjoy and which brings you happiness - kittens, puppies, unicorns, angels, life purpose, nature, wisdom, etc. Choose your deck of cards with this subject in mind.

When you buy any new set of cards, the excitement to start working with them is quite magical. But first, sit quietly, say your opening prayer and, when you are ready, remove your cards from their box. I like to cleanse my cards first before I look at them but whatever feels right for you. Then look at every card individually, putting your energy onto them. You don't need to spend a long time with this, just do what feels right. I do like to get to know my cards and this time is an ideal opportunity to do just that.

Now, I don't use any patterns or specific layouts when doing a card reading, I just pull whichever ones I am drawn to and also however many I feel appropriate for each individual reading. Even when I am doing card readings for other people, I get them to pull the cards they are drawn to and however many they would like. If you feel you would rather work with a structured pattern, there are sometimes suggestions for layouts in the back of the little book that comes with the cards. Try these and decide which way works best for you - there is no right or wrong way here, whatever feels right for you is right.

When you first start reading cards I would suggest you use a notebook for your results noting things like the date, the question asked, the names of the cards pulled and the messages you received. This will help you to get a better understanding of the cards and also build that trust with yourself, especially when you look back after a few days and realise that your readings made complete sense.

When you are reading for other people it is quite natural to feel a little worried about the messages you see or sense, and sometimes you may get the feeling that you don't want to tell them. But remember, you are only the messenger. The messages are not yours to keep and are nothing to do with you, and therefore do not have to make any sense to you. If you hold back giving messages for whatever reason, you will stop receiving messages. Spirit will simply stop working with you. Give whatever you get and new messages will continue to flow.

The more you can read for other people, the more relaxed you will be come.

HOW TO GIVE A CARD READING

1   Start by creating a calming environment and say your opening prayer. Centre yourself and become aware of how your body feels before you begin.

2   Ask spirit to move close to you and, when you feel connected, give your cards a good shuffle or mix up. You can mix them up in your hands or by moving them around

on a table; there really is no right or wrong way to do this. While you are shuffling, think about a question you would like to ask the cards or just think about what is going on in your life. Focus on your question, difficulty, challenge or your life that is happening now. Hold that question in your mind as you shuffle the cards.

3   Now spread the cards on the table in front of you or fan them out in your hand. Choose some cards you are drawn to, placing them face down on the table. You can either turn them all over at the same time and read them all together or turn them over one at a time and read them individually. Again, the choice is yours. This varies for me each time I do a reading. I have no set way and turn the cards the way it feels right for each individual reading.

4   As you look at each card, really look into the card. Connect with the card and see where your eyes are drawn. Whatever you are looking at ask yourself what it means to you in that moment. Pay attention to colours, shapes and objects. Look at what the people or animals are doing in the card. Get as much information as you can and pay particular attention to where your eye is being drawn to as this will be where the main part of the message is. If you have feelings, emotions, thoughts, smells, literally anything coming to you while you are reading the cards, know that these are all part of the reading. Do not dismiss anything and do not try to make sense of it in that moment. Gather all the information and, only when you have finished reading all the cards, will you

make sense of the messages. If it doesn't make sense in that moment, don't be disheartened, it probably will at a later date, especially when you are relaxed and not worrying about it.

5   When you have finished using your cards, make sure they are all the facing the same way, give them a final shuffle to cleanse them and place them in their box ready for next time. By getting in the habit of doing this after every use, the cards will always be as prepared as you are to start work.

6   Finish by thanking your guides for working with you and say your closing prayer.

If you are doing readings for a number of people, one after the other, and using the same deck of cards, the easiest way to cleanse your cards between each reading is to give them a good shuffle.   While you do this also ask your guides to break the link from the person you were reading for and connect you to the energies of the new person.   If you don't do this the chances are the cards will not make sense to the new person but will keep the energies of the last reading. Shuffling is also a great way to clear the energies between one question and another for your own personal reading or for the person you are giving a reading too. This is especially useful if there are a number of issues you, or they, want to explore with the cards.

By working with your cards as often as you can, you will not only build your confidence but will also build your connection and interpretation of the cards. The more you can work with spirit in this way the more precise and in-depth your readings will become.

CARD EXERCISES

1 Using the notes section of this chapter, pen and a set of Oracle cards, think of a question and give yourself a reading. Write the date, the question asked, the card or cards pulled and the interpretation you received. The more you do this the more connected you will become with your cards.

2 Each morning or evening, pull one card, making a note of it and seeing if it is relevant for that day. Do this for a week. At the end of the week, look at all the cards and see if there is a pattern or a theme that is trying to tell you something.

3 At the end of each week or month, look back at the notes you made for each of your readings. Do they make more sense to you now? Are you feeling a better connection with your cards?

4 Ask a friend or a family member if you can do a reading for them. Do it in the same way as you do for yourself, with the only difference being they touch the cards and not you. They can take notes during the reading if they wish. At the end of the reading ask for feedback. The more you can do readings for others the easier it will get.

5   *Ask a friend or family member to introduce you to someone you do not know and who is willing to have a reading with you.   Do the reading in the same way with only them touching the cards. Ask them not to give you any information that could help you with the reading.   Ask no questions, just ask for yes or no answers to make sure they can or can't take the message.   If they can't take the message, try and get some more information for them and if its still a no you will have to leave the message with them - it will normally make sense when they think through the reading afterwards. At the end of the reading, ask them for feedback.*

Doing more readings for people you know nothing about will help build the belief in yourself and your connection to your guides. This may seem scary at first but it is the best way forward to build this skill.

notes

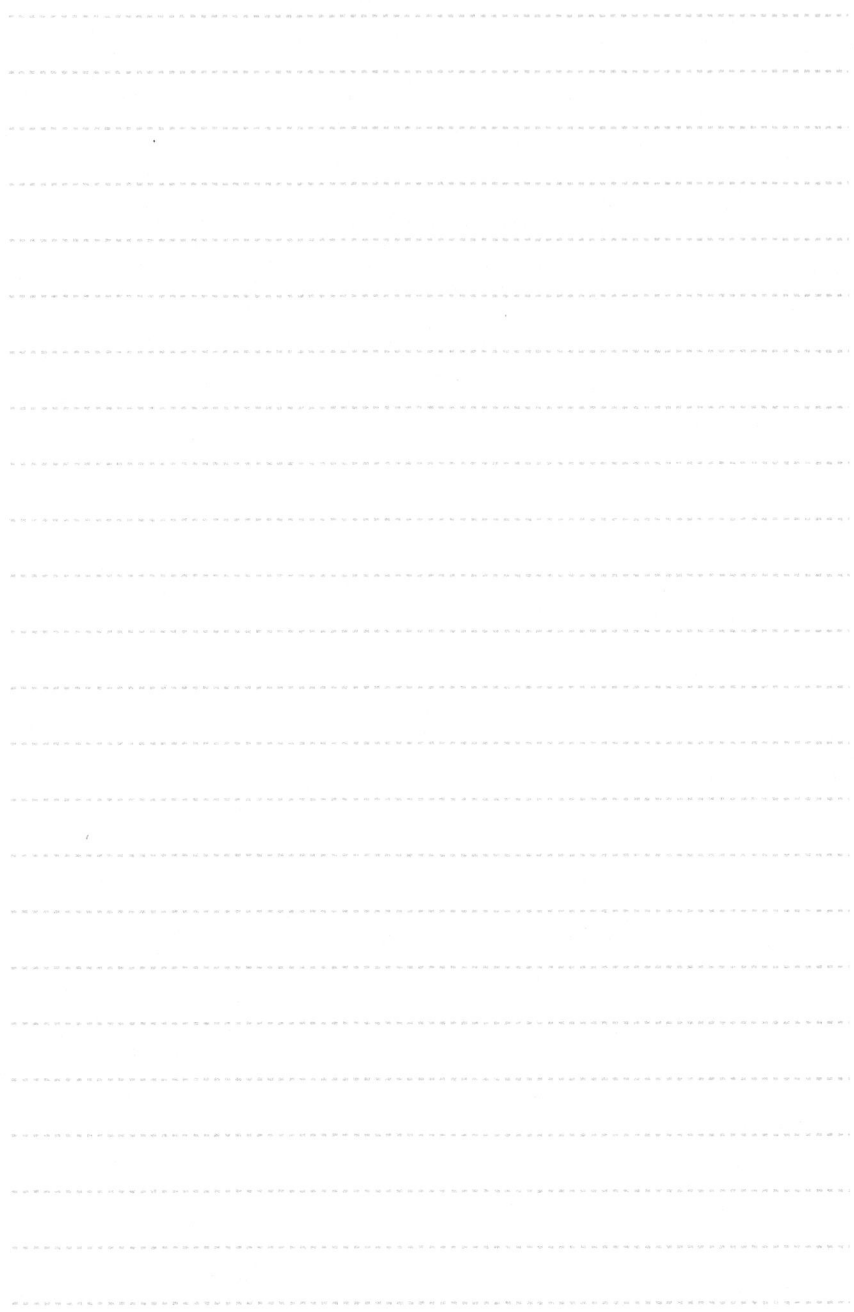

Chapter Nine
Lesson Eight - **CRYSTALS**

Everything speaks if you still your mind long enough to listen.

Using crystals can help to higher your vibration and bring a sense of calm to you, especially if you select a crystal that you feel drawn to, and then get an instant connection with.

Many people ask me which crystals should they buy and my answer is always the same - whichever you are drawn to. Crystals can have a tendency to find you and when that happens they become a very special tool. You will be drawn to any crystal that you need the energy of in that moment and when the time with that crystal is over, they can tend to disappear! Trust your own intuition with this and know that if it feels right then it is right. Sometimes our logical thinking can get in the way and then, we feel, we should be following the rules. But with crystals, especially, they have so many deeper layers, meanings and uses that enable each one to be used for multiple situations; therefore going with your gut instinct is normally the correct choice. Sometimes I like to pull a crystal from a bag filled with many different kinds of crystals, so I cannot see which I am drawn to - because I mostly go for the same ones when I see them! This allows me to use crystals I probably never would have chosen for a particular situation, and they are always correct. Experiment a little, which also opens up your awareness and intuition. Use this to start writing your own crystal definition book.

HOW TO START WITH A NEW CRYSTAL

When you get a new crystal, no matter where it has come from, start by cleansing it before you begin working with it. The reason for this is that the crystal will have collected many different energies from other people, wherever it has been, and a lot of these energies can be negative. Also they are energies you do not need in your environment or around you, so cleansing and clearing the crystal is a must for a fresh start with you.

You can then set an intention with the crystal by programming it to assist with specific tasks and projects, such as using it for healing, for meditation, to draw positive things to you, to help with your creativity, to attract abundance to you, or anything in-fact, to you. Just use the crystal as you feel drawn to do so in the moment.

It is a good idea to work with each new crystal on their own first so you can become fully aware of its energy and how you can use it. Carry it around with you for a few days and meditate with it. Once you have an understanding of it you can start introducing other crystals around it.

Be sure to cleanse the crystal and recharge it every few days or when you feel it necessary. A crystal will absorb energy as it works and, like you, needs a rest and a recharge from time to time. You may notice the crystal looking dull or not feeling as magnetic as usual and this could be the reason why.

Always cleanse your crystals after you have used them and before putting them away. This way they are ready to work the next time you need them and also this will keep them charged with their best energy to work with you for many years to come. For ways of cleansing see chapter twelve, although some crystals never need to be cleansed or recharged such as selenite and kyanite

ENERGISING

After cleansing your crystal, it now needs to be energised or recharged again, so that it can continue to release its own natural energies and vibrations.

There are several ways to do this but the ones I use are sunlight, moonlight and holding in the palm of my hand.

With each of these methods I say the same thing. I ask for the crystal to be filled with a blue light of positive energy to assist me as needed in any situation.

PROGRAMMING

Before starting, cleanse the room you are in of any negativity or unwanted energies. Be sure of what you want to program the crystal with and be ready with clear and direct thoughts. Choose a crystal that you feel drawn to and ask it if it is willing to work with you for this particular reason. By holding the crystal and focusing upon it you should be able to sense the answer.

When you are ready to begin, sit quietly, hold the crystal in front of you, focus on the crystal and clear your mind. Cleanse the crystal with a white light in your mind's eye and then concentrate on the specific energy you wish to program the crystal with - pushing the thoughts and energies from your mind directly into the crystal.

Do this until you feel happy that the required thoughts and energies have been sent into the crystal.

WAYS TO USE CRYSTALS

Meditation - Sit quietly with your chosen crystal in your hand or placed in front of you - I feel holding the crystal gives a stronger result but try both ways and decide for yourself. Close your eyes and focus your attention on your breath. Feel the energy of the crystal as this makes for a stronger connection. You can hold a crystal during any type of meditation whether it is guided or silent. Experiment with different crystals and different meditations with and without crystals and make a note of your results.

Create a crystal grid - Building a symmetrical pattern with crystals creates a strong energy inside the space. The grids can be small, to allow an intention to manifest, for example by placing a picture inside a crystal grid of someone who needs positive energy sent their way. It can also be a large enough crystal grid for you to sit in, allowing you to surround yourself with healing, guiding energy, which will remove negativity, give positivity and encourage growth in any area of your life. A variety of crystals can be used in grids, they do not have to be the same. Using different crystals together creates different and more powerful energies. As you build different grids, keep a note of the pattern and crystals used plus the reason for using the grid.

Hanging crystals - Crystals can activate positive energy or break up negative energy. They can also help by adding light and colour to areas that have chaotic energy. You can hang them in dark corners of your home where stagnant energy can accumulate and hanging them over a desk or work area can help improve concentration. Hang crystal spheres in your windows, which helps to disperse light out in many different directions for a fuller effect. Also, strings of multiple small crystals of different colours allow different energies to flow as needed.

For visualisation or manifesting - Use crystals for anything you are trying to manifest. By programming any crystal you are drawn to, it will enhance your visualisation. Some examples are,

amethyst for spiritual growth and inner peace - hold this crystal while meditating.

carnelian for creativity and motivation - carry this crystal in your pocket and place in your workspace.

citrine for prosperity and abundance - keep a small piece of this crystal in your wallet or purse.

obsidian for change - sleep with this crystal under your pillow and also hold a piece while meditating.

rose quartz for new relationship - keep next to your bed and also wear it close to your heart chakra.

tiger's eye for wealth - place this crystal on top of a written intention. By cleansing and empowering a pointed crystal with a flat base, this can help to hold the intention and create manifestation.

To give a reading - You can read crystals the same as any tool. The texture and grooves in the crystal add to the reading as does the colour and markings. Ask the crystal what message it has for you, then listen and pay attention to what your body is telling you. Look again at the crystal as you may see images in the crystal that you hadn't seen before. By placing a variety of crystals in a covered bowl or a cloth bag, your selection for the reading will be random and therefore appropriate for that moment, rather than picking a crystal your eye is attracted too. Although this way also works, we tend to keep choosing the same crystal which we like and also because we know how to read it and what to look for. We can also tend to go for the ones we feel, in our mind, will give the more positive reading for us.

Connecting with spirit - Meditating with crystals is a great way to connect clearly with spirit. Hold a clear quartz crystal in the palm of your hand or sit in a circle of crystals. You can ask your loved ones or spirit guides to move close and the energy from the crystals will enhance and quicken the connection between you.

Wearing crystals - For centuries people have worn crystals for protection and to use the energy from them. You can wear them in rings, necklaces, bracelets, earrings, or just carry them in your pocket, I have even known females to wear them in their bra! You can also place them in your purse or wallet. Remember to cleanse them often, especially if you have been wearing them all day and have been around negative people.

Using crystal wands - Healing wands are used to focus and direct energy to specific areas of the body. You can feel uplifted in their vibration just by holding the wand. The smooth round end is where you hold it, with this end facing towards you, and the pointed end you use to direct the energy. Usually the energy comes in through the rounded end and out through the pointed end. Then simply move the wand around your body as if you are brushing away something. Don't forget to cleanse the crystal wand afterwards. Selenite wands help remove negativity from your own aura.

If you feel you have some negative energy stuck, you can use the wand tip in a circular motion above the area in question, eventually pulling the negative energy out of your body. The round smooth end of the wand can also be used to massage the body, especially the soles of the feet. This helps to release tension while at the same time the wand's healing energy is transferred to the body.

For healing - NB Crystals do not take away anything from modern medicine. If you have a serious illness or complaint that has lasted a while, please seek medical advice.

All crystals give off energy and you will experience this the more you work with different ones. When you are feeling out of sorts, choose the crystal you are drawn to in that moment and the healing energy of it will be right for you.

Here are a few uses of the healing energies of some crystals that I have found to work for me.

When you have trouble sleeping, place a piece of amethyst either beside you or under your pillow.

If you have pain, place crystals on your body where you have the pain, such as amethyst on your forehead to relieve headaches.

Place a piece of orange calcite under your pillow to ward off nightmares and prevent night terrors.

Carry a piece of obsidian if you are overcome with negative thoughts.

Chakra work - Crystals can be used to open or balance your chakras. You can use any crystal to do this but if you know which chakra needs attention (you can use your pendulum to find out) then you can use a crystal in the correct colour for that chakra.

You can either hold the crystal in the area of the chakra which needs attention or you can lie down and place the crystal or crystals directly onto your body at the appropriate point of one or several chakras, then relax and allow the crystals to do their work. Laying a crystal on all your major chakras is a very healing and empowering experience. Remember to cleanse the crystals after use.

If you are unsure about chakras, chapter thirteen will explain more but here is a list of the chakras with their appropriate colour crystal and how they may help you.

base chakra - red crystals which bring you energy, courage, passion and love, plus also help with grounding, protection and manifesting.

sacral chakra - orange crystals which bring you joy, friendship and pleasure, plus also help with creativity, sexuality and physical desire

solar plexus chakra - yellow crystals which bring you enlightenment, optimism, warmth and clarity, plus also help with confidence, empowerment and willpower.

heart chakra - green crystals which bring you renewal, success in new ventures and good health You can also use the pink crystals on the heart chakra which help with love, emotions, relationships.

throat chakra - either blue or turquoise crystals. Blue crystals bring you trust, faith, patience and respect, while turquoise crystals help to centre and balance you, giving clear communication and honesty.

third eye chakra - indigo crystals which bring you wisdom, truth, dignity and spiritual mastery and also help with psychic abilities, vision and clairvoyance.

crown chakra - violet or purple crystals which help you with intuition, magic, dreams and imagination.

CRYSTALS AND THEIR MEANINGS

Using your instinct with a new crystal is the best way to get to know it and to feel in tune with it. I always like to meditate with a crystal I have not worked with before and get my own feelings on how to use it and what its energies can be used for. When I have made my own notes, only then do I look at the official meaning of each crystal - the results are always amazing. Try this way for yourself as it not only builds your confidence with using crystals but it also enhances your connection with them.

Here is a list of a few crystals I enjoy working with:

amethyst - helps to relieve stress and anxiety, mood swings and insomnia plus can help with meditation which can create calm and tranquility within you. Amethyst can also play a big part in opening us up to spiritual development, as it is an awakener of the third eyed and therefore helps to develop our intuition and spiritual awareness.

black obsidian - a spiritual protector which can help one to understand and face their deepest fears. This crystal acts as a protective stone that will ward off all kinds of negative energies, including physic attack, and absorbs negative energies from the environment. It is also the stone of truth. It will work like a mirror and allow you to see your own faults, mistakes and weaknesses, and then give you help in righting those mistakes and turning those weaknesses into strengths. If you find this crystal too powerful for you then use snowflake obsidian which is a gentler version of this crystal.

blue kyanite - it stimulates communication and psychic awareness on all levels. With its calming effect to the whole being, it is an excellent crystal to use during meditation and it also does align and balance all chakras.

blue lace agate - helps with communication especially in situations where angry words must be avoided but a clear understanding is necessary. It is an excellent emotional healing crystal as its healing properties work to melt away fear and anxieties.

carnelian - can help remove blocked or stuck energy which is stopping you from creating your dreams. This crystal restores motivation, confidence and happiness plus enhances creativity and sexuality.

citrine - for overcoming fear and maintaining a positive attitude. This crystal helps to build courage, assertiveness and raises self-esteem. It energises the body, sustains and supports physically and emotionally and it helps you to be present in the here and now. This is a crystal for success, money, abundance, and prosperity. Citrine doesn't hold any negative energy but emits large amounts of positive energy. It is a great crystal for manifesting and helps you keep a positive state of mind to dream big and attract everything you want in your life.

clear quartz - is one of the most versatile and powerful crystals for healing the spirit and programming clear intentions. It helps in clearing the mind and balance the body. It is great for changing negativity into positivity and it absorbs, stores, releases and regulates energy. By holding this crystal, it can encourage good health and healing.

emerald - a crystal of loyalty and domestic bliss. It enhances unconditional love, unity and promotes friendship. It opens and activates the heart chakra, having a healing effect on the emotions as well as the physical heart. This crystal brings harmony to all areas of ones life and helps to increase self-confidence and memory power *fluorite* - enhances memory, intellect, discernment and concentration and brings wisdom. It's an excellent all purpose healing crystal which promotes healing on all levels and also for self- love. It can remove blockages and narrow mindedness, bringing in new ideas and creativity.

green aventurine - helps to overcome fears of self-doubt and increase confidence and optimism. It can help attract new opportunities into ones life and help you to see the abundance and opportunities that surround you.

orange calcite - enhances creativity, energy and joy. It gets the positive energy moving which helps to increase confidence and boosts motivation plus encourages playfulness and lightheartedness.

jade - a crystal that can be healing and calming. It has a soothing purity about it, which purifies your energy field in a very accepting, loving and wise kind of way. Jade inspires and induces ambition toward the accomplishment of objectives

lapis lazuli - helps you go deep within your spirit to awaken your true destiny and divine purpose. It is said to stimulate wisdom, good judgment, truth and understanding. This crystal also helps with the process of learning by strengthening memory-based qualities. Use to develop psychic gifts and intuition.

malachite - known as the crystal of transformation, malachite helps bring energy and focus to new growth while clearing things which are holding you back. It clears and activates all chakras and is used for deep energy cleaning and bringing healing and positive energy.

hematite - a crystal for protection and grounding. It seals ones auric field against negativities as it helps to absorb negative energy, replacing it with a more positive vibration and calms in times of stress or worry. It is a very protective crystal and is great to carry to help you stay grounded in many situations.

pink tourmaline - activator of the heart chakra, this crystal creates joy and enthusiasm for life. It releases guilt, worry, depression and anxieties and guides those emotions into self-love. This crystal inspires love, happiness, spirituality and creativity and it can enhance your willpower.

red coral - it is believed to prevent ill fortune and bring prosperity and luck. It is a powerful crystal to use during meditation as it brings life force and positive energies.

red garnet - it cleanses and energises the chakras and ensures that energy is flowing smoothly throughout your body while helping to dissolve any energy blockages. It helps you to feel secure, safe and grounded.

red jasper - cleanses and stabilises the aura. It can give you the courage to speak your truth and have personal independence by helping you find your soul purpose. It brings vitality, tranquility and wholeness and can also inspire a positive attitude within you to give you the motivation to follow your dreams.

rose quartz - the love crystal which brings inner peace. It is a crystal of unconditional love, which helps to open the heart for true love and friendship as it brings nurturing, comforting energy. It also helps to heal the heart with forgiving others and also yourself. This crystal nurtures, supports and gives a vibration of love and compassion.

ruby - helps amplify positive energy and promote wealth and passion. Helps promote a clear mind, motivation and self-confidence.

selenite - helps with peace, purity and higher consciousness plus is often used to assist with meditation, as well as moving your spiritual growth forward. This crystal helps you to think clearly and has the ability to quickly unblock stagnant, stuck energy to promote a healthy, smooth flow of energy throughout your body. It is also used for good luck and protection.

sodalite - the awakener of the third eye which prepares the mind to receive the inner sight and intuitive knowledge.

tigers eye - a crystal which enhances personal power, integrity and the ability to bring heaven to earth. It brings order, stability, wealth and integration and has the power to focus the mind, promoting mental clarity and dispelling fear and anxiety.

topaz - it is known as a stone of love and good fortune. Topaz soothes, heals, stimulates, recharges, motivates and aligns the meridians of the body, directing energy to where it is needed most. It promotes truth and forgiveness and brings joy, generosity, abundance and good health.

CRYSTAL EXERCISES

1   Use different crystals while meditating and note your experience with each one. Do this every time you use the same crystal and see if the experience is the same. Note the time of day, how you are feeling both emotionally and physically as this can effect how the crystal works with you.

2   Meditate holding crystals and then meditate in a circle of crystals. Note the difference in the energies.

3   Ask someone to hold a crystal of their choice and after a few moments take it from them and give a reading as you would with any other tool. Ask them not to give any help during the reading but offer feedback at the end.

4 Create a crystal grid for manifesting something. Be clear exactly on what you want to manifest, feel the emotion of receiving it and then select the crystals you feel drawn to. Lay out the grid intuitively and when you are happy place a picture or have it written on a piece of paper what you want to manifest and place this in the centre of the grid. Or you can lay the crystals over the picture or piece of paper. Sit for a while, maybe meditating if you feel this will help.

5 Create a crystal grid to send healing to a friend, asking him or her first if this is okay. If possible, place a photo of

them in the centre, as this creates better focus for the energy. If you don't have a photo then write their name on a piece of paper and place that in the centre. After a day or two, ask your friend how he or she is feeling.

6 Place a crystal on top of a written intention. Allow it to do its work and record the result.

7 Start wearing or carrying a crystal with you each day and notice the way its energy works with you.

8 If you have an ache or a pain, randomly choose a crystal then place it on the affected area for as long as you feel necessary. State your intention that you will work with the crystal energies, allowing it to heal you in any way it can. After, make a note of how are you feeling.

9 Start writing your own crystal definitions in a notebook. Each time you use a crystal, write the name of the crystal, the reason you are using it, the feelings and emotions you feel from it and the outcome.

NOTES

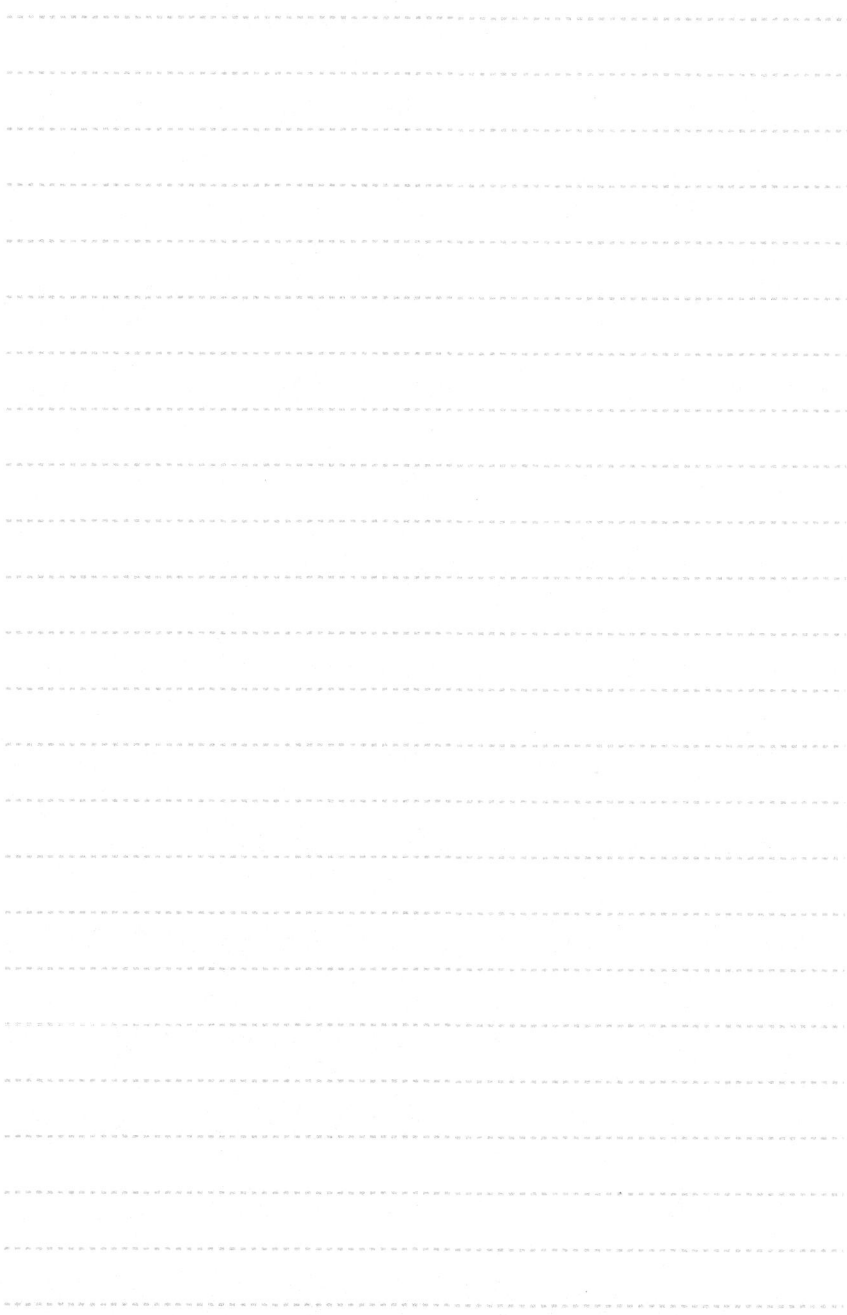

Chapter Ten
Lesson Nine - **SCRYING**

Scrying comes from the Old English word *descry* meaning *to make out dimly* or *to reveal,* and many of us have experienced scrying without even realising it. When you watch the clouds drift by in the sky and try to make out the shapes you see in them or while staring blankly at a wall or ceiling and you start to see faces or shapes move across, this is scrying.

Scrying is a form of divination, which means *foretelling the future,* but it is also a great tool to use for personal growth and guidance, not just for the future, but also for the present time as well as the past. You can find solutions to problems you are struggling with, learn more about your past lives, and see glimpses of the future too.

As with any form of divination, you are opening yourself up to spirit and it is always a wise choice to ask for protection before you begin. You cannot control what comes through to you, but your spiritual protectors can.

There are many ways of scrying, but the one I enjoy the most, and is quite possibly a popular choice, is looking into a crystal ball. You can use other reflective objects or surfaces and they can all help in showing you shapes or symbols that you then interpret what meaning they may have. Sometimes the message may reveal itself as a kind of movie with an entire scene being played out before your eyes. Whichever item you choose to use for scrying, it just serves as a focus for your attention and you still use your instinct and your spirit guides to help with messages, as you do with other tools.

Scrying is incredibly easy to do but it does take practice. Some of you may see things straightaway, but others may need to be patient as it can take many tries to master scrying. However it is for you, a little practice everyday will bring its rewards and before long you will be able to scry with little effort, no matter what you are looking at.

CRYSTAL BALL

Many different crystals are made into balls and there is no right or wrong one to use, although clear quartz is probably the best one to start with as you can see right into it. But choose whichever crystal ball you are guided to or experiment with different ones. Also the size of the ball does not matter which is helpful as they can be a little pricey the bigger they are. When making your choice, remember to be happy and connect to the crystal ball.

It is also a good idea to have a ring or stand to place your crystal ball upon while doing your readings, as this stops your hands from affecting the images you will get. Also use a plain black or dark cloth under the ball, which helps to concentrate your thoughts purely on the crystal ball. The crystal ball should always be wiped clean of fingerprints before being placed on its stand and then it is ready to begin work with you.

1 Prepare a dimly lit room with candles alight and burning incense, as these help to give movement of energy, but make sure there are no reflections from anything showing in the crystal ball.
2 Start with your opening routine, saying your prayer and asking your guides to move in close to work with you.
3 Get into a relaxed, meditative state, take some slow, deep breaths and, as you breathe out release all tension from your body while pushing thoughts from your mind. Do this for several minutes until all disruptive thoughts have vanished.
4 When you feel ready, place your hands around the crystal ball but without touching it, then close your eyes while you focus and feel the energy of the crystal ball allowing you to build a strong connection with it.

5 Now gaze into the crystal ball but do not stare, just allow your gaze to soften. Try not to blink too much, just relax, enjoy the peacefulness and simply gaze. Look at the aura of the ball, its energy, and allow your mind to be still. The images may appear in the crystal ball or in your mind's eye at first. Use your sixth sense here.

6 The crystal ball may appear to become cloudy like a fog or mist, which should then clear to show pictures or symbols. You then use your intuition to interpret what you see, sense or feel.

7 You can ask questions, or have no expectations, and just allow the images to flow.

8 If nothing happens then repeat the relaxation and preparation method. Perseverance is vital if the art is to be mastered. If still nothing happens, leave it for another day but keep trying.

9 When you feel the session is over, thank the crystal ball and your guides for working with you and say your closing prayer.

10 After use, keep your crystal ball wrapped up and out of direct sunlight.

11 Keep a scrying journal as this will help with the meaning of the symbols you see in your crystal ball. When you see something, think what it means to you and, with the help of your guides, you can build your own reference book for scrying.

WATER

The main principles apply to using water for scrying as using a crystal ball.

1 Half fill a bowl with water. A reflective bowl works well but a dark bowl allows you to concentrate better. Place a crystal in the bottom the bowl as this gives you something to focus on. Have a lit candle on either side of the bowl that will allow a gentle light over the water, but make sure their reflection does not appear in the water.

2 Begin with your opening prayer and ask your guides to move close to you.

3 Go into a trance-like state where you will feel peaceful, expanded, alert, focused and connected.

4 When you are ready, gaze at the water and allow your focus to soften. Images may come and go briefly but don't try to hold on to them or interpret them as this will make it harder to scry. Instead, allow all images and sensations to come and go freely while making a mental note of what you have seen.

5 Ask a simple question, when you feel focused and connected, such as how is tomorrow going to be? The images in reply might be literal or symbolic.

6 You can also drop pebbles in the water and interpret the ripples.

7 When you feel the session is over, thank your guides for working with you and say your closing prayer.

8 Reflect over what you have been shown and understand their messages.

MIRROR

If you have trouble finding the perfect mirror for scrying then here's how to make your own. Buy a picture frame the size and shape you like. Take the glass out and spray or paint one side black and repeat when dry. Place the glass back in the frame and hang on the wall in a quiet place where you will receive no distractions.

Using the same techniques as before, relax your vision and look into the mirror. You are trying to gaze softly while observing, not searching, stay focused on one point and wait for things to come through. When you first start, just look, don't ask questions, just allow the energy and messages to flow. Use your other senses as well to give an overall complete reading and be open to all information coming to you. After a while, images and scenes will begin to emerge. Watch until they fade and then interpret their message.

OTHER SUGGESTIONS

A piece of crystal - place the crystal in your dominant hand and hold it carefully over a candle flame and look for images or shapes within it.

A fire or a candle - the same principles apply when looking into a fire or a candle. Gaze at the smoke or flames as they rise up giving you spiritual messages.

Clouds - look at the clouds and observe the shapes they form.

You could even gaze at patterns in carpets or on floor tiles, anything which attracts your imagination.

SCRYING EXERCISES

1   Work with your crystal ball morning and evening for a week keeping notes on what you see, any questions asked and all interpretations of your feelings and senses. If you are not receiving anything from your crystal ball, keep going with this exercise until you do. Before you begin each session, tell yourself you will receive messages from your crystal ball today - and believe it!

2   When you feel connected to your crystal ball, use it every morning and ask it to show you something useful for your day ahead. Make notes on what you see but do not question or try to understand them. At the end of the day read your notes and interpret them.

3   Give a crystal ball reading for a friend. Give the messages you receive but ask for their feedback at the end of the session, not during, as this will allow you to stay focused with the energy of the crystal ball.

4   Using the above exercise experiment with some other ways of scrying, making notes of each one. You may enjoy another tool more or discover that one tool works better for different situations.

notes

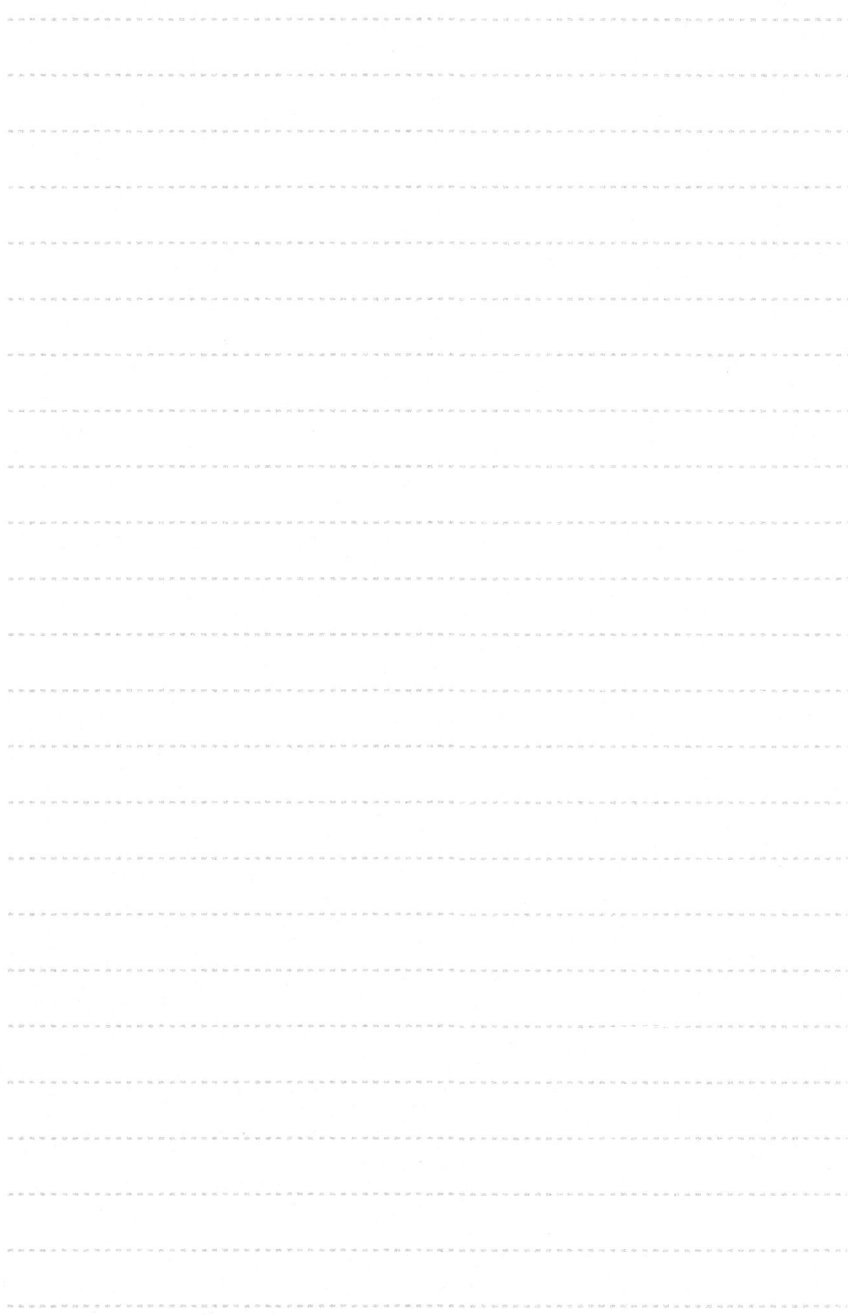

Chapter Eleven
Lesson Ten - **TEA LEAF READING**

Tea leaf reading or Tasseography, is an ancient divination method which began many centuries ago in China. The patterns of the tea leaves in a cup are interpreted to help give some insight to one's past, present and future. All you need are tea leaves, a tea pot, a cup and a saucer.

Most types of loose tea is fine for tea leaf reading, although try to avoid those which have large leaves, such as some green teas. The tea leaves in tea bags are not really suitable because during processing they become too broken down making them not as clear or easy to read.

Any cup is suitable but a nicely rounded cup, especially at the base so there are no corners as such, is preferable which allow the images to lay better for reading. The cup also requires a handle and a saucer.

If using a tea pot, it must not have a built in strainer as the tea leaves need to flow freely into the cup. You can add milk, lemon or a sweetener to your tea, if needed, as they won't affect the reading.

For the purpose of this exercise you will begin by giving yourself a reading

PREPARING FOR THE TEA LEAF READING

Make a pot of tea when you are reading for more than one person but for a single reading, you can put a pinch of tea leaves into a cup. Pour boiling water over them and then allow to stand for about three minutes.

Drink the contents of your cup, leaving tea leaves and about a teaspoon of liquid in the bottom.

Take the cup by the handle in your left hand and silently ask your question or ask for guidance about your future.

Swirl your cup three times in an anti-clockwise direction.

Then, place the saucer on top of the cup and carefully turn them both over, leaving them like that for about a minute, so all the liquid can drain away.

Now, gently turn your cup up the right way and the tea leaves are ready to be read.

HOW TO READ THE TEA LEAVES

Tea leaf reading does take practice, so don't be discouraged if this is challenging for you at first. It may look like the tea leaves are scattered in apparent confusion but after some concentration they should start to form lines, dots, small groups and even shapes. If you find it hard to make out the shapes, move the cup around and see if it makes sense from a different angle. Don't try to force anything, just allow the tea leaves to give you a true and honest reading. Be patient and search carefully for symbols, the more you look the clearer the symbols will become.

Begin with your opening routine, including your prayer.

Allow yourself to remain calm and centred and let go of any thoughts you have about the answers you hope the tea leaves will give you.

Holding the handle of the teacup close to you, look into the teacup.

Do any shapes or groups of leaves catch your attention?

Do any seem more important to you?

What is your intuition trying to tell you?

Divide the cup into sections

Traditionally, the tea leaves are read starting at the handle and moving clockwise around the cup.

The handle represents you, or the person who is receiving the reading, and you can see how near or far things are from you.

Any tea leaf shapes or groups that are close to the handle describe things effecting you now. It might indicate something on your mind or events you are experiencing.

Anything to the left of the handle is the past and is leaving your life.

Anything to the right of the handle is the present and your immediate future.

The Bowl of the Cup

Any tea leaves near the rim and the top third of the cup represents the present and will occur quickly, usually within days.

The tea leaves in the middle third of the cup are in the near future, usually a couple of weeks.

All the tea leaves in the bottom third and base of the cup are in the more distant future, possibly a month away.

In all three cases, the nearer the tea leaves appear to the handle, the sooner they will occur.

Reading the Tea Leaves

It is usually best to start with the largest shapes and work down to the smallest.

The more shapes there are in the cup the more important phase of life the questioner is experiencing.

Look to see if the shapes are spread out evenly throughout the cup or if they are concentrated in one of the sections.

The shapes should piece together to form a story. Observe the complete picture as a whole as well as the shapes individually.

Write things down as you go through your reading, noting both the shapes and your interpretation. The more details you add the better. By using your intuition you can build up your own library of symbols and their meanings.

If you get an answer you don't like, there is no point in going back and repeatedly reading the tea leaves as your reading will lose its accuracy and become muddled. Also you might start to misinterpret the tea leaves in an attempt to get the answer you want. It is better to just trust the reading and see how events play out.

Do not always expect the designs to be clear; they may sometimes be vague but use your own perception. Some symbols may contradict others but it is the combination of all the symbols and patterns that make the complete reading.

MEANINGS OF SYMBOLS

Here are some traditional meanings for a few symbols, but the best way to build a dictionary of meanings is by writing your own interpretations of what each symbol means to you. This will give a personal touch to your readings and, as your guides work with you, you will gain a quicker understanding of the symbols.

acorn = improved or continued health

angel = bearer of good news or a blessing coming

anchor = slow down or an end of a journey

ants = impending difficulties

apple = gain in business or achievement

arrow = a letter from the direction the arrow points

basket = a gift or a birth

bat = disappointment or fake friends

bell = a wake up call or unexpected news

birds = good luck. If flying, good news is coming. If at rest, a fortunate journey

broom = changes in life

butterfly = success and happiness

candle = assistance from others

cat = trickery, meanness or quarrels

circle = achievement and perfection or a wedding

clouds = impending upsets

cross = problems or ill health

dagger = envy or beware of a possible conflict

dog = friendship and faithfulness

door = unusual events

dots = lots of money

dove = good fortune

egg = fertility or new beginnings

face = setbacks

fan = flirtations

feather = inconsistency

fish = contentment

flower = a new love or wish granted

gate = opportunity

hammer = difficult work tasks

hat = better times ahead

heart = love, happiness or marriage

hill = obstacles

horseshoe = good health or financial improvement

hourglass = a decision should be made

iceberg = danger

key = new opportunities or solutions being revealed

kite = a wish will be granted

ladder = financial growth or improvement of a situation
leaf = future good luck
letters = initials of people or places
lines = progress or a journey - short line indicates a short journey, a wavy or broken line means a delayed journey, a straight line indicates a direct journey
mountain = challenges coming that you can overcome
palm tree = success and honour
pear = good fortune
profile = new friend
question mark = caution advised
rainbow = happiness
rose = success and recognition
shell = good news
ship = a successful journey
shoe = a change for the better
snake = hatred or a bad omen
spoon = friends will be generous
square = learn from your mistake and don't lose hope
star = good luck, great happiness or success
table = party time
tent = travel
trees = strength, ambitions fulfilled or help coming
triangle = wisdom or sharing your gifts
umbrella = annoyances
vase = a friend needs your help
volcano = keep your emotions in check
windmill = business rewards
wings = messages

TASSEOGRAPHY EXERCISES

1   Start by doing a tea leaf reading for yourself. If at first you feel you cannot make sense of the tea leaves, leave it for that day and go back to it the next day. Keep trying until you start to see the patterns and symbols. Stay positive and focused.

2   When you feel more confident with reading the tea leaves, start to ask questions and look for the answers in your cup. Keep a notebook of your questions asked and the symbols or patterns you saw in your cup. Make a note of what they meant to you in that moment.

3   Start building your own dictionary of meanings for the symbols and patterns you see. Draw each one exactly as you see it because the next time you see it, it could be showing in a different way. For example, a cat could be sitting in one reading and standing up in the next, each one giving a different message. Always be precise in your description and interpretation.

4   As you begin to master tea leaf reading and to gain more confidence, ask a friend to sit for you and read his or her tea leaves. Again make notes of the questions asked and your interpretation of the symbols seen and ask for their feedback at the end of the reading.

notes

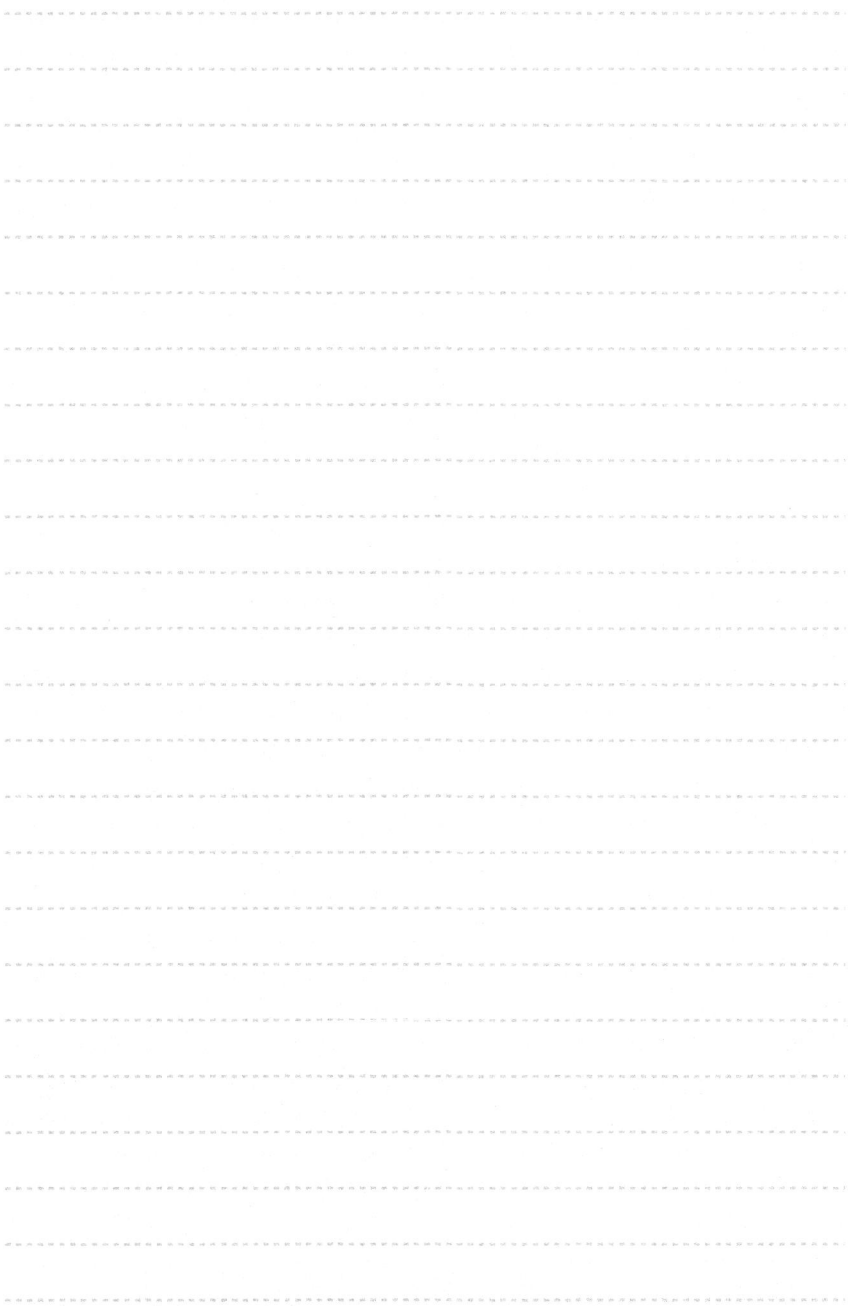

Chapter Twelve
CLEANSING

There are many different ways to cleanse things but I feel the intention of doing it is more important than being worried that you have to say or do a certain thing. Doing something is far better than doing nothing and you cannot do it wrong.

I am mainly going to refer to cleansing crystals in this chapter, but you can adapt all these methods to cleansing any thing.

You may be wondering what needs cleansing and why you should even bother. Well, everything you bring into your home will have gathered outside energies, many of which will be negative. To be sure that the energies are good energies and ones that you want to surround yourself with, you should cleanse new things so you can start afresh with them, knowing that the energies the item will attract will be from being around you. Your new crystals are more likely to be storing the most different energies of all the new things you bring home. If you never cleanse your crystals they will continue to collect energies until they are no longer useable or they will start to give the negative energy they have collected back to you, as that will be all they have to give. The reason that crystals are so effective in energy work is the same reason that cleansing them is essential - crystals pick up energy and give out energy. Cleansing your crystals resets their energy, so that every time you work with them, you are starting from a clean slate.

You can say your opening and closing prayer before you start your cleansing, especially if you have a lot of negative energy to clear. During any of these suggestions, in your mind or out loud, ask for the negative energy to be removed and then state what you want it replaced with, such as love and light or positive energy.

Here are some of the techniques I use to cleanse things. Some may resonate with you and others not so much but try them all and then use the one or ones that work best for you.

THE BREATH

Using your breath is the easiest way to cleanse smaller objects such as crystals and pendulums. You always have your breath with you and so it makes cleansing quick and simple, especially if something needs cleansing straightaway. A good example of this is when using a pendulum to balance chakras and then checking the chakras again straight after clearing that person's aura. It is best to cleanse it before the second use as the pendulum may have picked up some negative energy the first time around.

SUNLIGHT OR MOONLIGHT

Using the power of the sun or moon has an almost magical effect. Simply place your crystals outside, on your windowsill or any area that has enough sunlight or moonlight. You can leave them there for a few hours or up to seven days. The sun provides a stronger energy and the moon has a more gentle energy. Be aware that amethyst and citrine will fade over a period of time if left out in the sunlight for too long or too often. If you feel drawn to using this method for these particular crystals, try not to leave them out for longer than an hour or only place them in the sun just before sunset.

RUNNING WATER

Your cold tap water is the quickest way to do this but if you live by a stream, river or lake, holding the crystals in the flow of the water is a lovely way to cleanse them. Just hold your crystals under the running water and then allow them to dry naturally. You can enhance this method by visualising the water clearing out any negative energy and being flushed away. Do not cleanse calcite or selenite in this way as they will start to dissolve in the water.

UPON ANOTHER CRYSTAL

You can place crystals inside other crystals which allows any negative energy to be taken away. An amethyst geode works very well and a clear quartz crystal cluster is equally effective. Place no more than a few crystals onto the crystal points and leave over night or for up to 48 hours. These crystal formations have the ability to absorb the energies contained within other crystals, neutralise the energies and then release 'good' energy from the cluster back into the crystals being cleansed, so they effectively cleanse and energise at the same time.

SALT

Bury your crystals in salt by half filling a glass bowl with sea salt and then place your crystals directly into the salt. You can either bury them or leave them on the surface, which ever you feel drawn to do. Leave them for several hours, overnight or for a few days. After, your crystals should be rinsed under cold running water to remove any remaining salt. Do not reuse the salt, as it will have absorbed negative and unwanted energies.

FLOWER PETALS

This has a kind of exotic feel to it and is a cleansing method I only use very occasionally. Lay your crystals for 24 hours in or on a bed of rose petals, orange blossoms or honeysuckle to take away the negativity from them.

SMUDGING

This is a very popular way of cleansing anything and is especially effective when cleansing a room or house. This involves burning a smudge stick while walking around the room or house and asking for negativity to be removed and replaced by love and light. A feather can also be used to fan the smoke across the room and out into the corners where a lot of negative energy sticks.

When cleansing crystals or other smaller objects, lay them out and allow the smoke from the smudge stick to wash over the crystals and cleanse away the stored negative energies.

CANDLE FLAME and INCENSE STICK

Using a burning candle or incense stick works very effectively to cleanse anything. With the candle or incense stick in its stand, wave the crystal or item you want to cleanse through the smoke. Sage, sweetgrass, sandalwood and cedar wood are recommended for this because they effectively remove bad and negative built-up

151

energies. To cleanse a room, simply walk around the room holding the candle or incense stick extended out and paying particular attention to the corners of the room. At the same time ask for all negative energies to be removed and the area filled with love and light.

SOUND

You can use crystal bowls, Tibetan bells, Tibetan bowls, tuning forks, sacred singing, chants or healing music for this cleansing method. An easy way to cleanse a room, if you do not have any special tools with you, is to walk around clapping your hands and asking for all negative energies to be removed.

BURIED IN THE EARTH

Mother Earth recharges items with her vibrational energy. You do not need to bury them very deep, just enough to cover them but make sure you place a marker in the ground so that you know where to find them after 24 hours.

VISUALISATION

Visualisation is a beautiful way to cleanse anything and is a wonderful way to cleanse yourself. Sit in a chair and imagine a golden shower cascading down and around you from the source above. Ask that you be cleansed of any negativity and filled with calm and positive energy. Enjoy the sensation for as long as you need this peaceful experience.

To cleanse a crystal, or similar small object, visualise a bright white light coming from your third eye chakra, surrounding your crystal and sweeping all the negativity away. As the negativity leaves, it dissolves into nothingness. Keep doing this until you feel happy that the stored negative energies in your crystal have been flushed away and then visualise a blue light around your crystal energising it.

INTENTION

Hold your crystal in the palm of your hand and set an intention that the crystal be cleared of all bad energy. Blow that intention into the crystal and you're done.

At first you may want to cleanse your items and home on a regular schedule; on a full moon, or the first day of every month, are easy reminders for you. But as you develop a close connection, especially with your crystals and their energy, you will begin to sense when they need cleansing to release negativity they have collected and to recharge them with fresh light and energy. Also with your home and certain rooms, you will begin to sense when the energies change and it is time to cleanse them.

Remember that cleansing your crystals regularly will help keep them strong and powerful and their energy fresh for working with you. Also cleansing your place of work and home will help to keep you positive and focused.

Try the different methods of cleansing and take notes of what you cleansed and the results afterwards.

notes

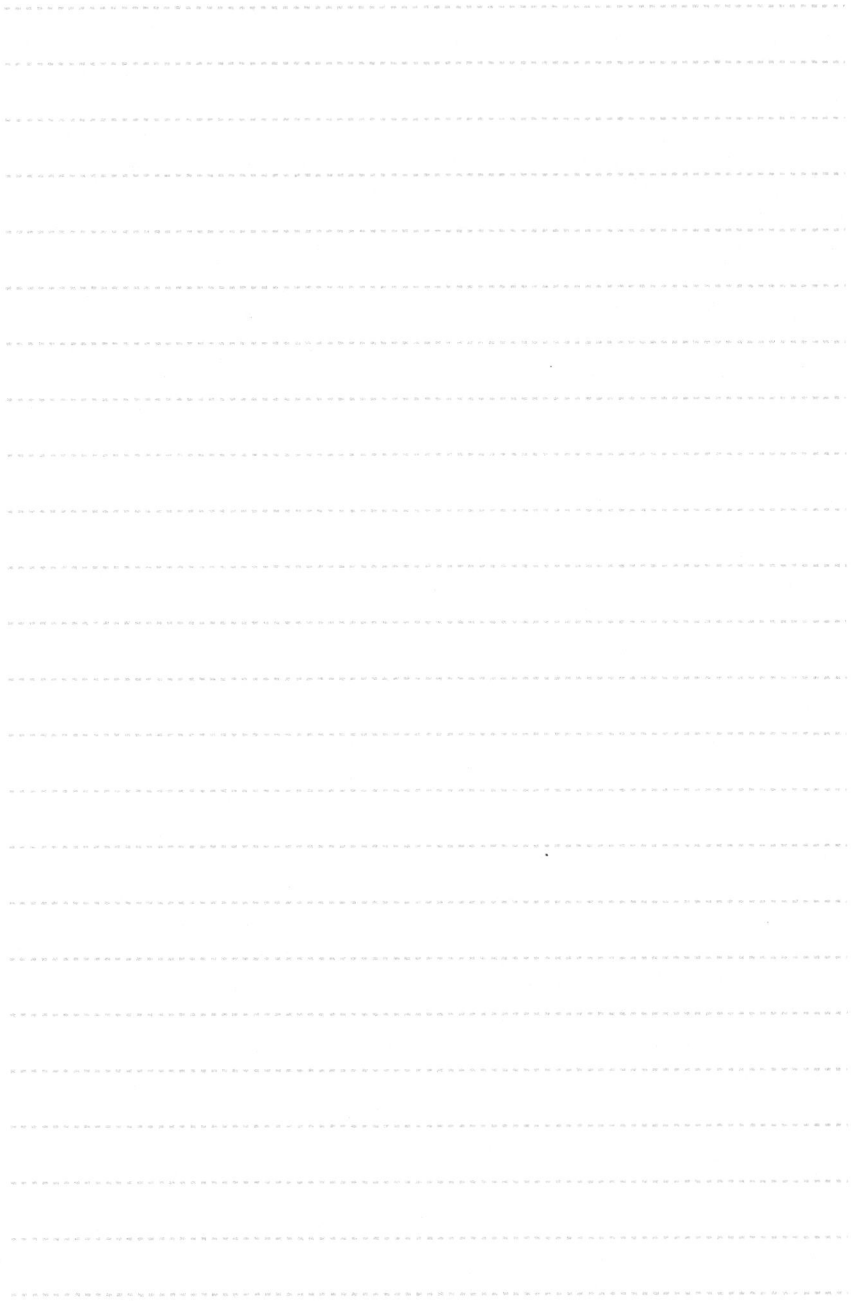

Chapter Thirteen
CHAKRAS

Chakra is an old Sanskrit word that literally translates to wheel. Your chakras are the life force that moves inside of you spinning and rotating and are called the centres of energy. The entire universe is made up of energy and your body is no exception.

There are seven main chakras in your body, which start at the base of your spine and move all the way up to the top of your head. In a healthy, balanced person, the seven chakras provide exactly the right amount of energy to every part of your body, mind and spirit. But if one of your chakras is too open and spinning quickly or too closed and moving slowly, your health will suffer.

By learning about the seven chakras you can become more in tune with the natural energy cycles of your body.

base chakra - located at the base of your spine.
Colour red.

This chakra promotes physical survival, vitality, stability, patience and courage. It connects all of your energy with the earth and helps ground you.

When unbalanced you will feel anxious and worried. You may also feel you can't concentrate and find yourself day dreaming your day away.

When balanced you will feel a sense of accomplishment and peace especially when you think about things like money and shelter.

sacral chakra - located below your belly button.

Colour orange.

This chakra promotes physical force, vitality and strength. It also generates new ideas, creativity, passion, endurance and sexual energy.

When unbalanced you may find yourself becoming addicted to things which are not healthy for you and feeling a sense of restlessness. You may also feel depressed and have a lack of passion or energy.

When balanced you will be happy in the pleasurable things life has to offer. You will feel inspired and happy and you will feel a sense of wellness and passion for life.

solar plexus chakra - located between your belly button and rib cage.

Colour yellow.

This chakra creates confidence, humour, personal power, authority, laughter and warmth within you plus helps to shape your identity and personality. This is where you feel your gut instinct and the area you feel strong emotions like love or fear.

When unbalanced you may feel the need to control others and be quick to get angry, with a lack of compassion or empathy. You may also feel indecisive, insecure, shy and needy.

When balanced you feel a sense of wisdom, decisiveness and personal power for yourself. You will have the confidence to win and achieve whatever your desires.

heart chakra - located in the centre of your chest.
Colour green.

This chakra deals with emotions and so it helps create compassion, love, understanding, sharing and forgiveness. Love for yourself and others.

When unbalanced you start to make unhealthy choices with love or putting others needs before your own. You may also find it hard to connect with others and don't allow anyone in.

When balanced you are able to feel love for yourself and for others without judgement and unconditionally.

throat chakra - located in your throat.
Colour blue.

This chakra helps you to connect to the world around you, affecting communication, self-expression and sound. It lets you speak your truth with clarity,

When unbalanced you may feel ignored and so you interrupt others and try to give yourself a louder voice or you shut down your voice and don't speak your truth. You may also feel unable to express your emotions or you struggle for words when you try to speak your truth.

When balanced you are able to speak clearly with love, kindness and truth and know exactly which words are appropriate for any situation, which then enlightens and inspires those around you.

third eye chakra - located between your eyebrows.
Colour indigo.

This chakra affects vision, intuition, psychic abilities, concentration, self-knowledge and insight.

When unbalanced you may become obsessed with psychic activities and be distracted from living a human experience. Or you may close off your third eye and ignore your own psychic experiences and become disconnected from spiritual experiences.

When balanced you feel in tune with both the physical world and the material world. You receive psychic information often and naturally but not enough to overwhelm you.

crown chakra - located at the top of your head.
Colour violet or white.

This chakra helps connect you to your spiritual self. It promotes imagination, inspiration and positive thought.

Achieving a balanced crown chakra is not easy to do and is the goal of every spiritual warrior. But it is the journey of attempting to achieve this balance that brings us happiness, good health and wisdom. By trying to balance this chakra it will also help to align and balance your other chakras. Instead of trying to open up and activate your crown chakra, focus on balancing the other six chakras. Meditate and connect with spirit and enjoy a balance of those activities with living and enjoying your human experience.

A JOURNEY THROUGH YOUR CHAKRAS

Start by sitting in a quiet, comfortable space where you won't be disturbed and say your opening prayer. Take a few deep breaths, allowing any tension and stress to slip away as you inhale and exhale. Now with steady breathing, let your mind be calm and just be in the moment with your body.

When you feel ready, bring your attention to your base chakra situated at the base of your spine and imagine a bright spinning red light. Feel it pulsing and rotating as you gently breathe. Stay there for a few moments absorbing the energy of the red light.

Now move your attention up to your sacral chakra, located just below your belly button. Sense a bright orange spinning light and feel the warmth of its glow. Notice for a moment how it moves with your breath.

When you feel ready, move your attention up to your solar plexus just above your belly button. Here you can sense the intense yellow light rotating. Stay with this energy for a moment.

Now move your attention further up to the centre of your chest where your heart chakra is. Here a bright green light spins. Connect with this energy for a few moments feeling the love.

Take your attention to your throat chakra and imagine a bright blue light spinning here. If you feel the need to swallow or clear your throat as you think about this area, go with it as it means it is starting to clear.

Next move your attention up to your forehead and your third eye chakra, just between your eyebrows. This area holds a deep indigo rotating light. Absorb the energies you feel here as it spins and becomes brighter.

Finally take your attention to the very top of your head and your crown chakra. Imagine a vibrant spinning violet light that is shining right out of the top of your head. This light is connecting you to the universe and as you connect with it, feel the peace it offers you.

When you feel that your body has absorbed enough of the energies from your chakras, ask that any remaining energy be sent out to where it may be needed in the universe. Allow your body to become calm and feel at peace, as you slowly bring yourself back to the room. Take a few deep breaths and when you feel ready, say your closing prayer.

BALANCING YOUR CHAKRAS

Keeping your chakras in balance helps you to stay happy and hopefully healthy. You can check your own chakras in a number of ways but here are two ways which are simple to do.

with a pendulum - After saying your opening prayer, hold your pendulum out to the side of you and with your other hand, place it over each chakra in turn asking the pendulum if the chakra is balanced as needed by you today. Remember the answer to each chakra and when you have checked them all sit with your hands palms up on your lap and ask your healing guide to balance your chakras as needed for you today. When you feel the energy has faded repeat the exercise and check each chakra again. Finish with your closing prayer.

You can also check your own chakras by holding your pendulum in the area of each chakra in turn and use the same question as above.

To check someone else's chakras the easiest and most accurate way is to have them lie on a bed and hold your pendulum over each chakra in turn. The pendulum may answer with your yes and no swing or, more often than not, it will spin in the direction the chakra is spinning. You can then tell how open they are by the speed of each spin. Now ask your healing guide to use you as a channel to balance the chakras as needed today.

With your hand - You can feel the energies of chakras with the palms of your hands, although this can take a little practice. Before you begin, get a good sense of how you and your body are feeling and then say your opening prayer. Place one hand about an inch above a chakra, tune in and you should start to feel the energy of the chakra in the palm of your hand. When you are happy that you are feeling the energy, ask your healing guide to balance that chakra as needed today. Repeat with each chakra in turn. After you have balanced all of your chakras you can go back over them individually, and get a sense of the new energy within them. Thank your healing guide and say your closing prayer. Make notes about how the energy of each chakra felt before and after the balancing and you can compare the process each time you do this. You can use this method on other people too.

Stay in tune with your body and how you feel day to day. Start by checking your chakras once a week and balancing them and make notes on how you were feeling before and how you felt after. As time goes by you will know when your chakras need attention.

notes

Chapter Fourteen
GROUP EXERCISES

Working with spirit is extremely rewarding and even more so when you can share your experiences and growth with others. Getting together with like-minded people once a week, or when you are able, is a good way to become consistent with your psychic development. It also offers you the opportunity to learn new things from each other, share ideas and experiences, plus ask questions about your thoughts and feelings.

Together with a group of friends the following exercises are fun to do, and talking about the end result of each one is a lesson in itself. You can adapt everyone of these exercises in many ways and I hope they will also inspire you to create more.

Enjoy and have fun.

PROTECTION

Before you meet decide who is going to lead the next group meeting. The nominated person should create a safe environment for everyone to work in. This person should be alert at all times and aware of everything that is happening with spirit, so that the rest of the group can feel safe, protected and relaxed to be able to achieve positive results with their psychic development. They will also open and close the group meeting with a prayer.

FEELING SPIRIT

1 One person in the group, I will use the name Eve, sits with her eyes shut and asks spirit to move close to her.

The rest of the group holds their hands up with their palms facing towards Eve while asking their spirit guides to send energy in Eve's direction.

In her mind, Eve accepts the energy and when she can feel spirit around her she can start to ask questions to find out who he or she is and if there is a message.

Sit like this for a few minutes until you all feel the energies drop.

Eve gives feedback to the group about her experience followed by any one else in the group who may also have something to share.

Repeat this exercise until everyone in the group has had a turn.

2 *For this exercise you will each need a pen and a piece of paper.*
Without telling the rest of the group, each of you thinks of one person you know who has passed.

One person in the group, I will use the name Tom, asks in his mind for his person in spirit to be brought through.

The rest of the group try to connect with him or her and write down all the information they receive, such as what he or she looked like, their name, where they lived, their job, how they passed, etc.

While the group is connecting and gathering information, Tom can also connect to his loved one and ask any questions he may have.

When everyone has finished receiving information, in his mind Tom thanks his loved one for visiting.

Now the group takes it in turns to share the information they received and at the end Tom gives feedback, explaining all about his loved one.

Repeat this exercise until everyone in the group has had a turn.

MEDITATION

1 The group leader reads a guided meditation to the rest of the group from chapter fifteen in this book. Throughout the meditation make sure everyone is safe. If you feel at any time spirit has moved too close to someone or someone is not safe, bring everyone back to the room in a slow and controlled manner, and end the meditation. Make sure the person you were concerned about is okay.

At the end of the meditation everyone takes it in turn to share their experience while the rest of the group helps to understand or interpret the messages received during the meditation.

2 Write your own meditation beforehand to use with the group.

PENDULUM

1 *For this exercise you will need a pendulum, a pack of playing cards and a tray.*

From the pack of playing cards, take out three cards such as the Queen of hearts, two of hearts and three of hearts.

The group leader shuffles the three cards and places them face down on a tray and then places the tray in front of someone in the group, I will use the name Eve.

Using her pendulum, Eve finds the Queen of hearts by allowing the pendulum to swing over each card in turn while asking a question such as "Are you the Queen of hearts?"

When Eve is happy with the answer she has received from her pendulum, she turns the chosen card over to see if she is correct.

Repeat this exercise until everyone in the group has had a turn.

To make this exercise harder, increase the number of cards placed on the tray.

2 *For this exercise you will need 8 pictures, 8 envelopes, pens, paper and pendulums.*

Before the group gathers, the group leader writes down all the names of the pictures. He or she then shuffles the pictures before placing one into each envelope, which have been numbered 1-8.

The group each has a pen, piece of paper and a pendulum.

The group leader reads out the list of picture names, in no particular order and everyone in the group writes the names on one side of their piece of paper.

Each member of the group takes one envelope and using their pendulum finds out which picture is in their envelope and then writes that number by the appropriate name.

When everyone is ready, pass the envelope you have been working with to your left and repeat with this next envelope.

Continue until you have a number by all of the picture names on your piece of paper.

At the end, the group leader opens the envelopes one at a time to reveal the answers.

3 *For this exercise you will each need a pendulum, pen and piece of paper.*

Pair up in your group, one person sits on a chair and their partner stands.

The person standing, I will use the name Eve, uses her pendulum to see if her partner's chakras are balanced, I will use the name Tom.

Standing beside Tom, Eve holds her pendulum in one hand and out to the side so it can swing freely. She places her other hand in the area of Tom's chakras, reading each one in turn.

Starting at the base chakra, Eve asks her pendulum if the chakra is balanced as required by Tom today. After making a note of the answer, she works her way up the remaining chakras, asking the question and making a note of the answer.

While Eve is checking the chakras, Tom sits quietly. When completed Eve shares her results with Tom.

Now Eve stands behind Tom and places her hands upon his shoulders. Eve asks her healing guide to step forward and, using her as a channel, sends healing energies to Tom balancing his chakras as is necessary for him this day.

Tom, sitting in the chair, accepts the healing and closing his eyes, relaxes and enjoys the experience.

Eve should feel some energy moving through her hands. If this doesn't happen do not worry, it is not essential but with practice she should start to feel energy.

Stay like this until either the energy starts to fade away or you feel the time is right to stop.

Eve thanks her healing guide for working with her and then asks Tom how he is feeling.

Eve now checks Tom's chakras in the same way as she did at the start of this exercise and writes down her results.

Eve and Tom now give feedback to each other.

When the group has all finished the exercise, each pair shares their experience with everyone in the group.

AURAS

1   Start with two people from the group, I will use the names Tom and Eve.

Tom stands facing a wall with his back to the group. Eve stands on the other side of the room opposite him.

With her hands up in front of her, palms facing towards Tom, Eve very slowly starts to walk towards Tom paying particular attention to the sensations in the palms of her hands.

As Eve gets closer to Tom she should begin to feel his aura. She should notice a slight pressure in her palms.

After moving a little more into Tom's aura she can then stop.

Now Eve gently bounces Tom's aura by moving her hands backwards and forwards.

Tom should say when he can feel Eve walk into his aura and he should feel this pressure pushing him backwards and forwards.

The group leader should make note of the distance at which the aura was felt and how close Eve needed to get before Tom felt the sway of his aura.

Switch people until the entire group has experienced both positions and then compare notes.

How do the people who have smaller auras differ from the people who have larger auras?

2 Choose one person in the group whose aura you will all look at, I will use the name Eve.

The rest of the group looks at Eve's aura, that could be seeing it or getting a sense of knowing what it is like.

Discuss what you each are seeing such as the colour and size of her aura.

The group leader asks Eve to think of something that makes her feel very sad. As she does this you should see her aura change.

As a group, discuss the changes you see happening. Eve's aura should shrink around her giving a strong protection, and also the colour could change too.

Now the group leader asks Eve to think of something that makes her feel extremely happy.

Again as a group, discuss what you see. Eve's aura should start to expand with a colour change.

Allow everyone to take a turn at this exercise.

3 *For this exercise everyone will need a pen and paper.*

Choose one person in the group whose aura you will all look at, I will use the name Tom.

The rest of the group will look at Tom's aura and with the information you will gather from his aura, from your guides and the feelings in your body, you will write down a reading for Tom, adding your name at the bottom.

When everyone has completed their reading, take it in turns to read them to Tom. Allow Tom to give feedback at the end of each one.

Repeat this exercise until everyone in the group has received their readings.

PSYCHOMETRY

1   *For this exercise you will each need an object which belongs to you, such as a piece of jewellery or something meaningful to you.*

Each person in the group holds their object and then passes it to the person on their left.

Taking it in turns, you each connect with the item you have received and then give a reading out loud for it.

The owner of the item gives feedback.

Repeat until everyone has connected and given a reading for the object they have received.

2   *For this exercise you need to plan ahead and ask everyone to bring an object to the next meeting and show it to no one in the group.*

All members of the group place their object in a covered basket or bag, so you can't see what others have placed in there.

Take it in turns to choose an item from the container, making sure by touch that it is not your object.

Connect with the object and give a reading.

At the end of the reading, whomever the item belongs to make will make themselves known and give feedback.

Repeat the exercise until everyone has had a turn.

3   *For this exercise you need to plan ahead and ask everyone to bring a photograph to the next meeting of a loved one who has passed.*

Someone from the group, I will use the name Eve, without saying anything, passes her photograph to the person on her left.

Taking it in turn, everyone connects to the photograph and gives any information that comes to them.

After everyone has read the photograph, Eve can now give feedback and the history of the person in the picture, either confirming or explaining what each of the group had said.

Repeat the exercise until everyone has shared their photograph.

CARDS

1   *For this exercise you will each need a pen, piece of paper and a set of oracle cards.*

One person in the group, I will use the name Eve, asks a question out loud to the rest of the group.

Using their set of oracle cards, the group each pulls a card for Eve. After connecting with the card, their guides, and noticing sensations in their body, they write the message they have received on a piece of paper.

177

When everyone is ready, take it in turns to go around the group, each person shows the card they pulled and reads the message, with Eve giving feedback.

Repeat this exercise until everyone in the group has taken a turn to ask a question.

2 *You will each need a pen, piece of paper and a set of oracle cards for this exercise.*

Everyone in the group is given a large sheet of paper and they write their name at the top. Folding the paper over, so the name cannot be read, the group leader gathers the papers, shuffles them and then hands them out randomly to the group.

Using a deck of oracle cards each, everyone pulls a card for their piece of paper and writes the message, starting near the fold and remembering that the whole group has to write their message underneath.

After you have written the message, write the name of the card plus your name, fold down the paper to cover the message and everyone passes their paper to the person on their left.

Repeat by pulling a new card each time for the new piece of paper until everyone has written one message on each piece of paper.

Now take it in turns to unfold a piece of paper, read the name at the top and then read out the list of messages, getting feedback each time.

3 *For this exercise you will need a deck of playing cards and a set of oracle cards.*

One person will be the reader, I will use the name Tom, and will be reading the oracle card.

The group leader takes enough cards from the deck of playing cards to match the number of people left in the group making sure that one of these chosen cards is the joker.

The group leader shuffles these chosen cards and offers them unseen to the rest of the group who each pick one, but doesn't look at it.

Tom shuffles the oracle cards, chooses one and gives a reading.

At the end of the reading the group looks at their chosen card and the one who has the joker is the one Tom has been reading for.

The person reveals himself or herself and gives Tom feedback.

Repeat this exercise until everyone in the group has give an oracle card reading.

CRYSTALS

1 *For this exercise you will need a selection of crystals.*

Everyone in the group chooses a crystal and holds it during a meditation.

At the end of the meditation, and after everyone has shared their meditation experience, each passes their crystal to the person on their left and one at a time, takes it in turns to read the crystal passed to them.

After each reading, the owner of the crystal gives their feedback.

2 *For this exercise you will need a selection of crystals in a bag.*

One person from the group sits with their back to the group, I will use the name Eve.

Without Eve knowing who, the group leader offers the bag of crystals to someone else in the group, I will call this person Tom.

Tom picks a crystal from the bag and the group leader hands it to Eve.

Eve connects with the crystal and gives a reading.

When Eve has completed the reading she returns to the group and Tom gives feedback.

Continue with this exercise until everyone has had a turn at reading a crystal.

3 *For this exercise you will need a selection of crystals.*

The group leader places a chair in the middle of the group and creates a crystal grid around it.

One person from the group sits on the chair, I will use the name Eve, while the rest of the group sends energy to her. Eve, with eyes closed and relaxed, accepts the energies.

The rest of the group holds their hands up with their palms facing towards Eve while asking their guides to send energy in Eve's direction.

If Eve has any ailments, she can ask for pain to be removed from an area, or she can ask one of her spirit guides to step forward, or ask anything that she would like to know. The crystals will enhance her experience plus the energies of the group.

When the energy has faded, the group leader asks Eve is she is feeling okay.

Eve gives feedback to the group about her experience and anyone else can also share any information they received for Eve.

Repeat this exercise until everyone in the group has had a turn to sit in the centre chair.

SCRYING

For this exercise you will need pens, paper and a crystal ball.

Each person in the group writes three different questions they would like answered onto three separate small pieces of paper. Fold them up and place all the questions in a bag or bowl.

Take it in turns to pick a question and read it out loud to the group. Without knowing who asked the question, get the answer from looking into the crystal ball.

When the message has been completed, the person who asked the question makes themselves known and gives feedback.

Keep taking it in turns until all the questions have been answered.

If you pull your own question, place it back in the bag without reading it out to the group.

TASSEOGRAPHY

For this exercise y*ou will each need a pen, paper, cup and saucer. Plus a tea pot, tea leaves and milk if required.*

Make a pot of tea and each drink a cup then prepare your cup for reading, see chapter eleven.

Each person writes their name at the top of a piece of paper and then passes the piece of paper and the cup to their left.

Read the cup you have just received from the person on your left and write your message at the top of the piece of paper followed by your name and then fold the paper down, covering up your message. Please note that everyone in the group will be writing their message on this sheet of paper so keep your writing small.

You all again pass the cup and the piece of paper to the left and then read the cup you have received.

Keep repeating this until the correct cup and piece of paper gets back to its original owner.

Now take it in turns to read the messages out loud and give feedback to everyone in the group.

notes

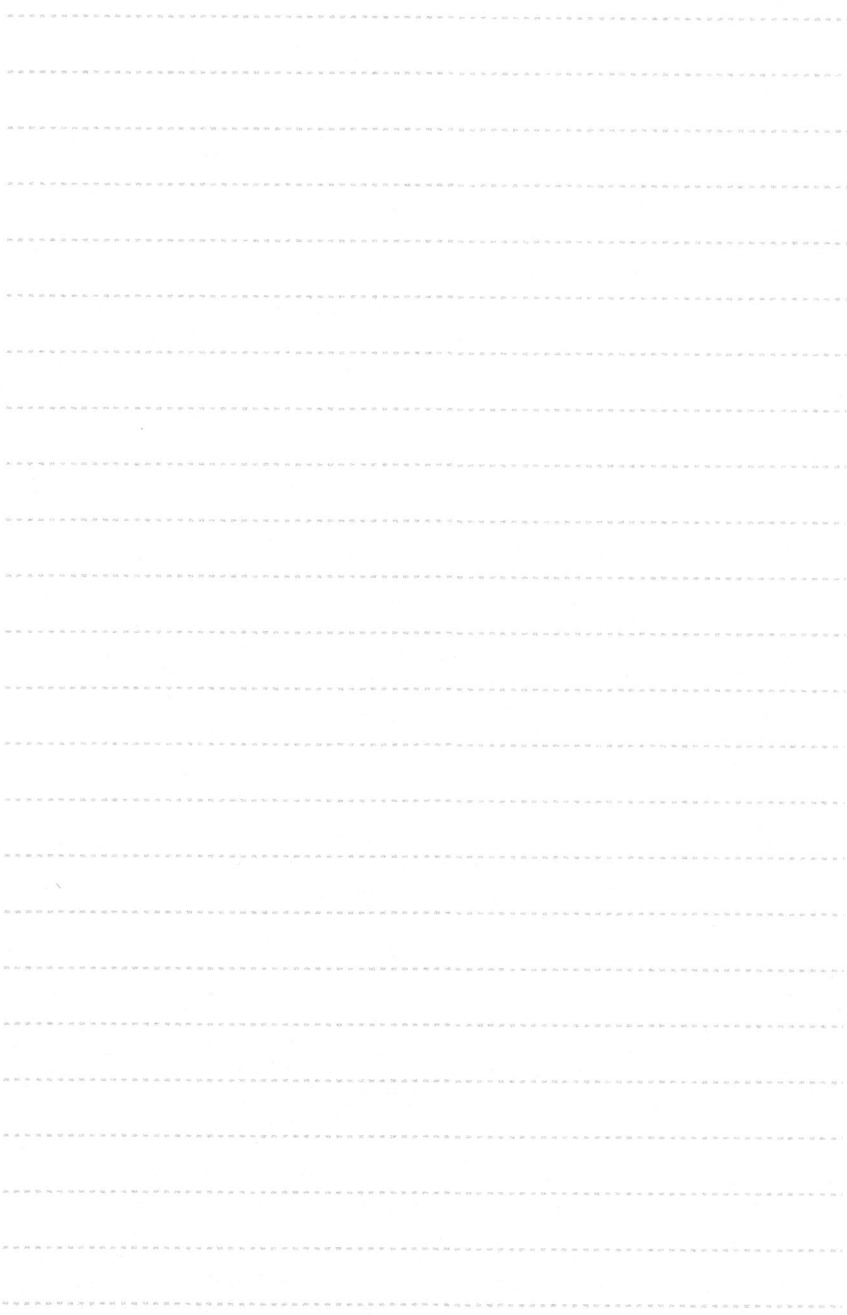

Chapter Fifteen
MEDITATIONS

Here are some guided meditations you can use in your groups. Read the meditation aloud in a slow and gentle voice while the group closes their eyes and follows the journey. Create pauses in your reading, to allow the listener to take their time following you, as they journey through the meditation. As you read the meditation, also keep an eye on the group and watch for any strange happenings which may occur, such as spirit moving in too close to someone or someone becoming upset. At anytime you can bring the meditation to a close by bringing everyone back to the present moment, slowly and calmly.

At the end of every meditation, look around at everyone to make sure they are back from their experience and are feeling okay.

When everyone is ready to continue, go around the group asking each person in turn about their meditation experience. They can share all or part of their journey, depending on how they feel.

Meditation 1 - *The Gift of A Talisman*

Sit comfortably with your hands in your lap and palms facing up, place your feet on the ground and close your eyes.

Take a deep breath in and, as you exhale, feel your body start to relax.

Take another deep breath in and as you exhale, you feel your shoulders and arms relax.

Now, with nice steady breaths, allow any thoughts you may have to drift slowly by, as you relax a little more.

You are lying on a beach by a calm sea.

It is a beautiful sunny day but the beach is empty except for a few seagulls.

The peace and quiet is exactly what you need after your busy day.

You begin to notice a few gentle sounds - the birds flying past as they play together and the occasional gentle wave stroking the sand - these are just background noises, a gift from above, letting you know you are alive and well.

As you lie there, enjoying the warmth of the sun, you suddenly notice a different sound in the waves as they roll in towards the shore.

You sit up and watch as the waves carry with them a large wooden box which they leave on the beach not far from where you are.

Standing up, you move towards the box, which resembles a large treasure chest with the familiar curved shaped lid.

You notice the lid is slightly open and, as you open it wide, you see it is full of wonderful things and has a sign saying 'PLEASE TAKE ONE'.

Without hesitating, you sort through the treasures until you find one that is full of positive meaning for you.

You know it is a talisman that will restore your spirits whenever you feel low.

You pick it up, close the lid of the treasure chest and return to where you had been lying on the beach.

You sit with your talisman for a few moments, allowing the energies to flow over you.

It is now time to leave the beach and to come back to this room.

You are aware of my voice and the noises in the room.

You are aware of sitting in your chair.

You are aware of your arms and your hands, your legs and your feet.

And, when you are ready, open your eyes.

Meditation 2 - *Bringing Peace To Your Life*

Sit comfortably with your hands in your lap and palms facing up, place your feet on the ground and close your eyes.

Take a deep breath in and, as you exhale, feel your body start to relax.

Take another deep breath in and as you exhale, you feel your shoulders and arms relax.

Now, with nice steady breaths, allow any thoughts you may have to drift slowly by, as you relax a little more.

Imagine your everyday life.

What does that look like to you?

It could include the alarm clock going off, getting to work, traffic jams, phone calls, deadlines, and hustle and bustle.

Now imagine you are walking down a city street.

Gradually you notice that there are fewer people and only a couple of cars, less noise and no hustle and bustle.

You turn the corner and the buildings come to an end.

All that is left are a few rustic cottages.

Ahead of you lie meadows and woods.

There is long grass, wild flowers, hedges and trees.

Birds fly overhead.

You wander along, breathing in the sweet air.

Then you lie down on the grass and rest.

It is time now to slowly walk back to the city.

You can cope with the demands in your life because your rural paradise lives on inside you.

You can revisit it whenever you want.

It is time to come back to this room.

You are aware of my voice and the noises in the room.

You are aware of sitting in your chair.

You are aware of your arms and your hands, your legs and your feet.

And, when you are ready, open your eyes.

Meditation 3 - *A Year From Now*

Sit comfortably with your hands in your lap and palms facing up, place your feet on the ground and close your eyes.

Take a deep breath in and as you exhale, feel your body start to relax.

Take another deep breath in and as you exhale, you feel your shoulders and arms relax.

Now, with nice steady breaths, allow any thoughts you may have to drift slowly by, as you relax a little more.

In your mind's eye you see a large golden pyramid coming down from the main source above you.

It slowly comes down, eventually covering you completely.

You are sitting in this golden pyramid on a comfy chair.

In your hands you are holding a ball of white sparkling light.

You throw the ball of white sparkling light towards one wall of the pyramid.

As it lands the white sparkling light disappears and a door appears.

You walk towards the door and open it.

You do not go through the door but instead you stand and look out.

What you are seeing before you is your life one year from now.

It is time to close the door and return to your comfy chair, thinking about all you have seen.

Now the pyramid rises slowly back up to the source.

As you watch it leave, you know you can use it at any time to see the different stages of your life, with the knowledge that you can change your path at anytime.

Slowly bring yourself back to this room.

You are aware of my voice and the noises in the room.

You are aware of sitting in your chair.

You are aware of your arms and your hands, your legs and your feet.

And, when you are ready, open your eyes.

Meditation 4 - *Gaining Strength*

Sit comfortably with your hands in your lap and palms facing up, place your feet on the ground and close your eyes.

Take a deep breath in and as you exhale, feel your body start to relax.

Take another deep breath in and as you exhale, you feel your shoulders and arms relax.

Now, with nice steady breaths, allow any thoughts you may have to drift slowly by, as you relax a little more.

Imagine you are at the top of a mountain.

The view is magnificent but you are not feeling as on top of the world as you would like.

Next to you is a sparkling stream.

As you glance down at the stream you feel the urge to get into the water.

Feeling safe and knowing that you are guided by spirit, you are now lying in the stream.

In fact, it feels as if you are the stream.

The water cleanses your body and calms your nerves.

You relax back into the water and feel yourself floating down stream at a gentle pace.

Gradually the landscape changes from mountain to woodland and then to pasture.

The stream turns into a powerful river, pushing everything along with it.

You start to feel more powerful, more directed and more aware of how much you can achieve.

As the mighty river flows into the ocean, you become conscious of life's limitless possibilities.

There are no boundaries except those that you set yourself.

Feeling that nothing can stop you from achieving your goals, you open your eyes and discover you are still at the top of the mountain.

You look around at the magnificent view and realise that you feel on top of the world.

It is time to come back to this room.

You are aware of my voice and the noises in the room.

You are aware of sitting in your chair.

You are aware of your arms and your hands, your legs and your feet.

And, when you are ready, open your eyes.

Meditation 5 - *Manifesting Your Desire*

Sit comfortably with your hands in your lap and palms facing up, place your feet on the ground and close your eyes.

Take a deep breath in and as you exhale, feel your body start to relax.

Take another deep breath in and as you exhale, you feel your shoulders and arms relax.
Now, with nice steady breaths, allow any thoughts you may have to drift slowly by, as you relax a little more.

In your mind's eye, you see yourself in the forest on a beautiful summer's day.
You see the trees covered in leaves.
You hear the birds singing.
You can smell the fragrance of the wild flowers.

You begin to walk through the forest enjoying the beauty that surrounds you.
Eventually you come to a large clearing and you see a big old tree to one side surrounded by green grass, which is filled with daisies and buttercups.
You sit down on the soft cool grass, beside the tree and rest your back against its old trunk.
The tree fills you with strength and happiness.
As you sit here you start to imagine something you would like to manifest - something you want to happen.
Imagine that it has already happened.
Picture it as clearly as possible in your mind.

Now in your mind's eye, surround your desire with a pink bubble - put your goal inside the bubble.
Pink is the colour associated with the heart, for unconditional love and nurturing, and it will bring to you only that which is in perfect affinity with your being.

Now let go of the bubble and see it floating off into the universe, still containing your vision,

It is free to float around the universe, attracting and gathering energy for its manifestation.

As you watch it float away, I'll leave you to spend a quiet moment gathering more strength and happiness from the tree.

It is time to leave.

You stand and hug the tree.

You turn and walk back through the forest feeling so grateful for the abundance you already have in your life.

It is time to come back to this room.

You are aware of my voice and the noises in the room.

You are aware of sitting in your chair.

You are aware of your arms and your hands, your legs and your feet.

And, when you are ready, open your eyes.

Meditation 6 - *Absorbing Energy*

Sit comfortably with your hands in your lap and palms facing up, place your feet on the ground and close your eyes.

Take a deep breath in and as you exhale, feel your body start to relax.

Take another deep breath in and as you exhale, you feel your shoulders and arms relax.

Now, with nice steady breaths, allow any thoughts you may have to drift slowly by, as you relax a little more.

In your mind's eye, look at your base chakra.

Sense whether it is working to your benefit.

Fill your base chakra with the colour red.

Now look at your sacral chakra.

Sense how it is working for you.

Fill your sacral chakra with the colour orange.

Now check your solar plexus.

Get a sense of how this is working.

Fill your solar plexus with the colour yellow.

Next check your heart chakra.

Sense whether it is working to your benefit.

Now fill your heart chakra with the colour green.

Now check your throat chakra.

Sense how this is working.

Fill your throat chakra with the colour blue.

Now check your third eye.

Sense the energies here.

Fill your third eye with the colour indigo.

Finally check your crown centre.

Sense the energies here.

Fill your crown chakra with a beautiful gold colour.

Now ask your healing guide to move close.
Ask that each chakra is balanced to the need of your energies in this moment.
As your guide begins to work with you, see your whole body covered with the golden energy radiating down from your crown chakra.
You absorb the energy from the golden cascade and feel warmth and love all around you.

As you feel your healing guide move away from you, you whisper "thank you".

Now the golden energy starts to fade but you see in front of you a mist.
As the mist moves closer to you, you begin to see a figure emerging.
As it steps forward you recognise a loved one.
They move beside you and you take this opportunity to ask questions, receive guidance and absorb the energy and love from them.

Now is the time to say your goodbyes and for your loved one to return to the mist and disappear.

You now check your chakras and see the colours have faded leaving you feeling energised and happy.

With the messages from spirit in your heart, you slowly return to this room.

You are aware of my voice and the noises in the room.

You are aware of sitting in your chair.

You are aware of your arms and your hands, your legs and your feet.

And, when you are ready, open your eyes.

notes

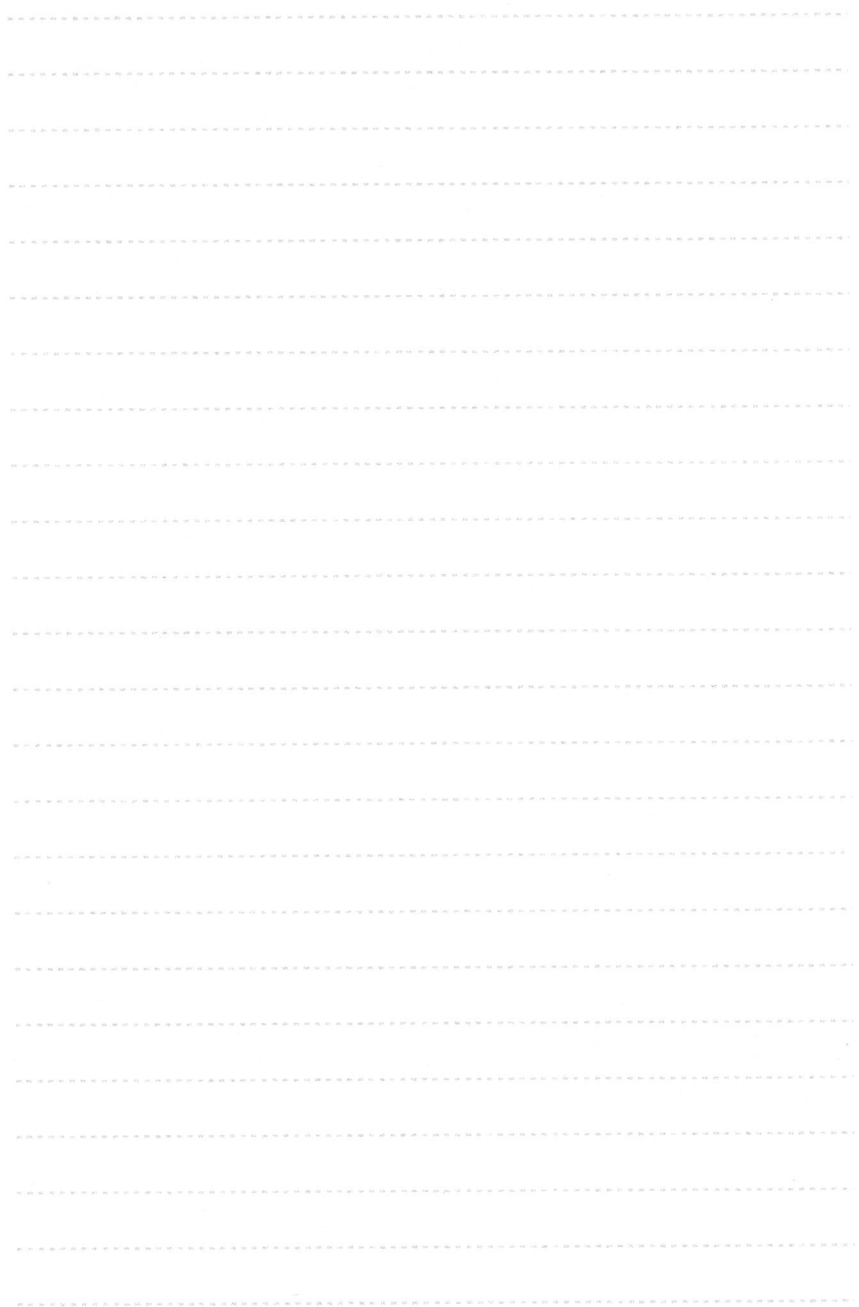

Tranquil Spirits

I hope you have enjoyed working with this book. If you have any questions, or would like to learn more, please don't hesitate to contact me. Your journey with spirit is important to me, and I would love to hear about your progress.
Hugs and smiles.
Jacqueline

email: mytranquilspirits@gmail.com
website: www.tranquil-spirits.com

Printed in Great Britain
by Amazon